CATS

500 QUESTIONS ANSWERED

hamlyn

CATS

500 QUESTIONS ANSWERED

Dr David Sands

First published in Great Britain in 2005 by
Hamlyn, a division of Octopus Publishing Group Ltd
2–4 Heron Quays, London E14 4JP

Distributed in the United States and Canada by
Sterling Publishing Co., Inc.
387 Park Avenue South, New York, NY 10016-8810

ISBN 0 600 61179 5
EAN 9780600611790

A CIP catalogue record for this book is available from the
British Library

Printed and bound in China

10 9 8 7 6 5 4 3 2 1

Notes
The advice given here should not be used as a
substitute for that of a veterinary surgeon. No cats
or kittens were harmed in the making of this book.

Contents

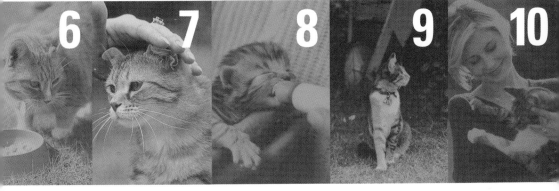

Introduction

Cats, by their nature, will always cause us to ask questions. A cat is caught in the headlights crossing the road in the darkness ahead: what makes its eyes reflect and glow? Is it a black cat and, if so, will it bring us luck? Why did it give us that strange, grimacing look? Why does my friend's adopted cat knead, suckle and pluck at my woollen jumper, and purr like a miniature motorbike? The answers to a host of questions about cats have been brought together in this book. I thoroughly enjoyed writing and researching it – if any reader has a question not asked here, you will find contact details on page 256 and I will do my best to answer it. Numerically, cats are now the number one domesticated pet around the world. Is this related to their predisposition for aloofness and natural independence? They are not just much more independent than dogs, they are also more politically correct. Cats are rarely caught fouling pavements or playgrounds – felines are much too secretive for that. They rarely attack people going about their business, and even more rarely cause anyone serious injury.

The truth is that cats are a popular companion animal because they are a practical pet. They are ideal for working people, college students and those who are at home a great deal, sometimes isolated from family and friends, or for the elderly and frail. In contrast to the near-silent cat, a nervous dog is often excessively vocal when left 'home alone', barking itself into a frenzy and disturbing neighbours to distraction until its owner comes home. Compare that picture with the one of a contented cat that is more or less able to take care of itself during daytime hours. Conveniently, cats are happiest sleeping off the previous night's adventures during the day, usually beside a warm radiator or on a comfortable bed.

Owners, and the rest of the world, may not always be aware of what their cats are up to. The secretive character of felines means they prefer to hunt, prowl and copulate at night, but this also means that they are difficult to monitor, even for those who are motivated to observe their movements. Cats are able to slip in and out of houses, hedgerows, gardens, undergrowth and woodland with little sound or indication that they have ever been there.

Cats are magical, mysterious, mythical and magnificent to those who cherish them. (They are murderers, menacing and mendacious to those who do not.) In this book, cats are much-loved moggies and adored, bejewelled pedigrees; they are valued equally as commoners and as aristocrats by their owners. Enjoy this book, and take all the pleasures from it that you can – it was a pleasure for me to write. And I always had a soft spot for Cat Woman. I wonder why?

Dr David Sands

Cats: Fact and Fiction

Are all cat breeds and the 'big cats' related, from the tiger to the tabby?

Yes: all cats, large and small, are related to each other. Scientists working on the relationship of animals place 'genetically similar' feline species, from the family known as Felidae, into four groups.

1 Cheetahs

2 Panthera group

The Panthera group includes the best-known large cats such as lions, tigers, leopards, jaguars, lynx, bobcats, pumas, and others not so well-known such as the flat-headed cat, fishing Asian cat and the newest cat to be discovered, the onza.

3 Ocelots

4 Wild cats

The last two groups include wild forest, jungle and desert cats, as well as domesticated cats. According to DNA evidence, it would appear thatall four groups share a common evolutionary ancestor.

Going back further in geological time, there is also fossil evidence that suggests there was a common ancestor linking the three main land-based carnivores – felines (cats), canines (dogs, wolves, jackals and foxes) and ursi (bears) to each other.

What makes cats and dogs so different from each other?

One of the main differences between cats and dogs lies in their behavioural development. The majority of felines are solitary predators that hunt alone, although lionesses and cheetahs are notable exceptions. The majority of

THE EVOLUTION OF THE CAT

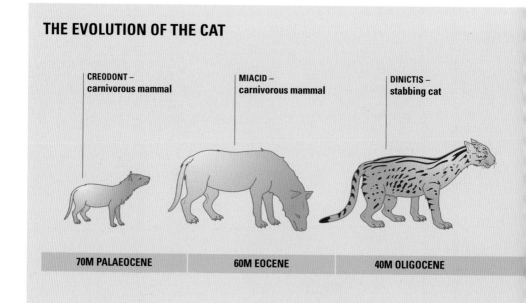

CREODONT – carnivorous mammal

MIACID – carnivorous mammal

DINICTIS – stabbing cat

70M PALAEOCENE   60M EOCENE   40M OLIGOCENE

canines, including wild dogs, hunt in groups or packs, the European fox being the solitary exception.

This fundamental difference between felines and canines means that cats are mostly solitary animals whereas dogs are group or social animals. This means that their behaviours are therefore very different. It is also one of the major reasons why house cats behave in a different way around humans to the way dogs behave: cats are not actively seeking a 'social structure', whereas dogs – in the absence of a canine pack – have adapted to accept their human family as a replacement 'pack'.

RIGHT Cats and dogs shared a common ancestor that evolved several million years ago into two groups, solitary and pack predators.

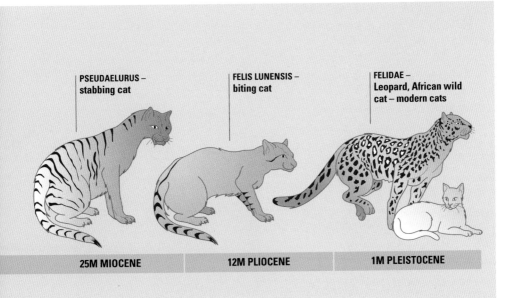

PSEUDAELURUS –
stabbing cat

FELIS LUNENSIS –
biting cat

FELIDAE –
Leopard, African wild cat – modern cats

| 25M MIOCENE | 12M PLIOCENE | 1M PLEISTOCENE |

Where did the domesticated cat originate?

Domestication of the cat is thought to have begun in the ancient Middle East. It is highly likely that the Egyptians encouraged wild cats to inhabit their massive grain storage barns in order to keep down the numbers of vermin such as rats, mice and locusts.

Most researchers conclude that the origins of our domesticated cats belong with the African wild cat *(Felis libyca)*. However, when scientists make comparisons between the African and the Scottish wild cats *(Felis sylvestris)*, they have discovered that there is very little – apart from their attitude towards humans – to separate these two naturally tabby-striped cats. Some scientists believe the two species may represent the complete range of one, single species. However, while the Scottish wild cat is recorded to be extremely shy of humans and is almost impossible to tame (even when crossed with domesticated cats), the African wild cat has displayed a willingness to associate with humans.

According to some authors and researchers, there may have been a role in the taming of wild cats for the jungle cat *(Felis chaus)*, because cross-matings with domesticated cats and this species have produced cats that prove very adaptable to people.

What is the relationship between house cats and wild cats?

There are two major forces that helped to shape the domesticated cats we know today.

1 Genetic Despite the many generations between the house cat and the wild African or Eurasian animals, the same instincts have been carried faithfully gene-by-gene along the DNA trail. This dictates all physiological and most behavioural developments, including skeletal development, reproduction, agility, coat and eyes, plus parental care and feeding.

2 Human beings For thousands of years, we have bred cats and distributed them around the world in ways that suit our purposes.

Genetically, there is little to separate the domesticated house cat we know today from the wild cats found in temperate regions. The tabby house cat shares the general body shape and stripy coat pattern of its wild cousin, and they look very much alike. It is the feral cat

RIGHT The ancestry of the domestic cats we know today lies in the wild cats, including the African wild cat.

(semi-wild offspring of domesticated cats) that gives the house cat's ancestry away: in behaviour terms, wild and feral cats are much more instinctive, secretive and nocturnal than the tame, domesticated cat.

What are the main differences between the wild cat and the pet cat?

Working and house cats have shared their lives with humans for thousands of years. In doing so, they have adapted to become less fearful and more interactive with us. **Domesticated cats** Walk down any busy street or drive down country lanes in the evening, and you will see representatives of the domesticated cat population; they are not difficult to observe. Domesticated cats interact with us, 'marking' us, 'possessing' us and demanding to be fed by us, without the same instincts to avoid and mistrust another 'predator' that exist in wild cats.
Wild cats In sharp contrast, observing wild cats in nature requires immense patience and research in order to counter their secretive and nocturnal habits. Territories and movement patterns have to be recorded by motion-activated cameras, and areas monitored for signs of physical and scent 'markings'. More is known (and has been filmed) about the wild cat litter-mother hunting, and protecting and moving her kittens, than about the solitary, secretive males. They prefer to compete, hunt and mark territories at night, and go about their lives almost invisible to the human beings around them.

Why do cats' personalities vary so much?

A cat's personality depends entirely on the DNA passed on by its mother and father, modified by the learned behaviour and environmental circumstances of its birth and early life. As it grows from a young kitten into a cat, everything that is learned from the litter mother from birth onwards, plus the environmental circumstances that surround its initial development, affects the personality of a cat.

There could be arguments about the exact percentage influence, but at least 75 percent of personality and behaviour is probably instinctive and less than 25 percent learned.
Feral cats At one end of the scale, a kitten born to feral parents, beneath the ruins of a old barn, will certainly have its instincts 'sharpened' from birth. This kitten will soon learn how to hunt for food, distinguish prey types and avoid potential predators. Such a kitten will always be aware of what is going on around it, and may even appear to be 'crazy' or permanently anxious or nervous (hyper-alert) when it is brought into a home.
Domesticated cats In complete contrast, a kitten that has been born in the comfort of the washroom kittening box, tucked into a warm blanket with a litter mother that is fat and content, is hardly likely to care which side its cream is poured. Life for such a secure kitten is entirely about food, sleep and play, and interaction with humans quickly becomes second nature.

How many cats are there estimated to be in the world?

The total cat population in the world is thought to be about 200 million. The greatest cat numbers can be found in the USA, where 25 percent of the total population is known to reside. The graphs below show a sample of cat populations around the world, and the ratio of cats to people in a selection of countries.

CAT POPULATIONS

Country	Number of cats (millions)
Britain	7.5
Canada	2.7
China	46.8
France	8.7
Germany	6.5
India	3.9
Italy	7.0
Netherlands	2.3
Poland	5.4
Russia	12.5
Spain	2.8
USA	75.0

CAT / HUMAN RATIOS

Country	Ratio of cats to people
Austria	1:1
Britain	1:10
Europe (overall)	1:4
India	1:500
Taiwan	1:500
USA	1:4

What does it mean when cats are described as 'territorial'?

Territorial animals are those with a strong instinct to live within fixed land or aquatic boundaries. As small, solitary predators, cats have evolved to live within a fixed land space that is large enough to support them in terms of prey but modest enough for them to defend. In the wild, this territory is within a jungle, forest, rural or desert habitat. In these environments, wild males will compete with each other and attempt to mate aggressively with any sexually mature female cat that strays into their chosen territory.

Cat territories overlap and several males may consider the same area to belong to them. At the point of encounter, the strongest of the two will successfully challenge for the 'territorial rights' and eventually chase off the rival. The smaller the area he has to defend, the better the chance of the cat being successful.

House cats consider their home, yard, garden and surrounding boundary markers such as fences, walls, trees and any freestanding structures to be part of their territory. In some instances, this may extend to surrounding streets or lanes. Research has suggested that house cats may operate a 'time-sharing' form of understanding, but a strong-willed, physically fit individual will usually roam unopposed across territories. When other cats 'invade' a perceived territory, a house cat is often able to retreat into what is usually the most secure part of its territory – the home.

Do cats live in groups in the wild?

The answer is 'not usually'. In spite of this, there are instances where cats – normally solitary, territorial predators – will congregate together to form unnatural groups. This is often the case when feral cat groups live in an area where there is a high cat population but limited source of prey. Obviously behaving against type, these cats may congregate around waste-disposal grounds hoping for food scraps, or in urban streets or derelict buildings where they are being artificially fed.

Natural aggression is often significantly reduced among large groups of cats. This may be due to the numbers being so high that it is impossible for dominant cats to assert themselves over individuals. In this situation, the bullied cat can more easily retreat and become lost in the group.

ABOVE Cats are naturally solitary animals and would not normally live in groups. They are independent animals and enjoy their own company.

What is a 'tom' cat? And what is a 'queen'?

The names given to un-neutered cats relate to gender. An entire or uncastrated male cat is known as a 'tom'. A 'queen' is a female that has not been spayed or subjected to a hysterectomy.

Why is there so much superstition about cats?

In contrast to many other nocturnal animals, cats are generally thought to move about in mysterious ways. Many nocturnal animals are linked to mythology, legends, moralistic and magical tales, and fairy stories. The owl is a perfect example of the link between nocturnal animals and humans, in that mythology has associated it with attributes such as intelligence and wisdom, and also characterized it as a carrier of news.

There is also something about the colour black, a successful colour with feral cats that has always been associated with magic. Thriving in darkness, being dark and being busy at night is what witches and magicians are all about.

People living alone find cats a comfort and tend to encourage 'detached cats' to take up residence in their homes. Reclusive individuals, especially females, have always been viewed as odd, and in some regions and historical periods were quickly categorized as hags and witches. By association, cats belonging to a recluse would be seen as an extension of their personality and ways. The word 'familiar' was strongly associated with cats and witches from medieval times and indicated that they could change from one into the other. It was common for any blame or misfortune to be directed at reclusive individuals and their companion animals.

There have been so many interpretations of the light in cats' eyes, their amazing survival skills and the 'demonic' sounds of mating cats that it's not difficult to understand why they encourage mythologizing. The beliefs about them have led to cats being buried within walls, tortured and banished through the centuries.

In contrast, there have also been times in history when cats were thought to be harbingers of good fortune, with the ability to ward off evil spirits.

Did the ancient Egyptians really worship cats?

It is known that the Egyptians believed cats had some kind of divine association. The recovered contents of burial chambers and hieroglyphic writings in and around tombs have proved that cats, far from being simply useful working predators of vermin, were also integral to the life and spiritual beliefs of every class of people at the time. No other known civilization has afforded cats such high status.

Evidence reveals that young temple cats were frequently mummified and this, along with the many statues, ornaments and illustrations discovered, confirms their importance in Egypt over all other countries. Cats were also given a direct fertility association in the cat-like goddess Bast. She was known to have a strong association with Egyptian women and could help bring happiness in relationships and births.

All the great Egyptian dynasties encouraged their people to worship the sun and every aspect related to its daily cycle of sunrise (birth) and sunset (death). Cats became drawn into sun worship because of the reflected light apparently captured in their eyes. This distinctive characteristic, caused by a special retina adaptation known as the 'tapetum', helped to fuel the idea that cats could somehow retain some of the sun's powers on Earth.

The priests of the day held cats in such esteem that much ritual and religious ceremony involving them was developed and brought into the daily lives of Egyptians. Many laws existed to protect cats and ensure that their burial after death was dignified, and that rituals carefully followed the sacred teachings related to them.

Are cats mentioned in the Bible?

There is no direct mention of cats in the translated Bible. It is known that the Israelites distrusted everything associated with the Egyptians, who ruled over them. The fact that the Egyptians held cats in such high esteem (see page 16) encouraged the occupied population to despise them almost as much as they hated the occupiers, so this may be the reason why they are not mentioned in the Bible.

ABOVE **The cat was sacred to Bast, the Egyptian goddess of fertility . Bast was sometimes known as Pasht, and it has been suggested that this is a possible origin for our word 'puss'. Originally models of the goddess showed her with a lion's head but from around 1550 BCE she was shown with a cat's head. Cats were kept in her temple at Bubastis on the Nile.**

ABOVE Feral cats are domesticated by association with humans but revert back to semi-wild instinctive behaviour.

good or bad luck. The strong Hallowe'en association in the USA that continues to this day has influenced Americans to think of black cats as having a connection with witches and bad luck. Conversely, in Britain a black cat crossing your path is usually associated with the arrival of good luck.

Superstitions and cats go almost hand in hand, and much of this has to do with the ups and downs of religious ideology. On the one hand, cats were persecuted by the Catholic Church in the Middle Ages and were viewed mainly as agents or familiars of the devil and witches. On the other hand, cats have been worshipped and admired over a 3,000-year period for their links with magic, for having many lives, for being able to 'catch the sun' (see page 17) and for bringing good fortune.

Whichever side the cat was on at the time, it has always managed to attract controversy, fear, admiration and obsessive attention. There can be few, if any, direct comparisons with other animals in this respect.

Why is it believed by some that cats bring good luck, and by others that they bring bad luck?

This depends on which side of the Atlantic you live or lived, and in which century. Sighting a black cat, for example, can be interpreted as either

Are cats naturally (or always) more active at night?

In the wild, cats would be most active between dusk and dawn. The main driving force behind this is the search for prey:
- Cats' preferred prey – rats, mice and other small mammals – are usually more active at these times.
- Birds and land mammals often roost or rest during the twilight and night

hours, making them more vulnerable to a night-time predator.

- For cats, the daylight hours are about resting and building up energy for nocturnal activities. In times of food shortage, or when territories are shared with other cats, an individual cat may be driven to hunt, compete and mate in the daylight hours, but this would be the exception rather than the rule.

During the centuries of domestication, the division between night and day has been artificially blurred by candle, fuel, gas and electric lights, and by human-dictated mealtimes, presence and general activity patterns. A house cat will adapt its activity to suit the human cycle, because more often than not it is advantageous to do so. Nevertheless, instinct drives a cat to be the nocturnal animal it has evolved to be. This can be seen when house cats cry or even wail to be allowed outside at night more than at any other time.

What is a 'feral' cat?

The term feral, from the Latin *firal*, *ferus*, *fera*, is used for plants and animals that have reverted back to nature. In connection with felines, the term is used to identify a domesticated cat that has partially regressed back to the wild. This usage dates back 400 years and (perhaps coincidentally) is similar to *feralis*, a Latin term for anything pertaining to funeral rites and the dead. Perhaps this is another reason why cats are associated with witchcraft and matters of life and death.

Is it true that some cats enjoy water and like to swim?

Most cats loathe water and react to it with panic and distress. However, there is one cat, the Turkish Van, that is fast becoming famed for its swimming talents. Equipped with a fine, dense coat and neck ruffle that thickens even more in the winter months, this breed will happily plunge into water. There are Turkish Van individuals that do not enjoy water and this against-type behaviour could be due to the fact that several generations back even these cats would rarely be exposed to a lakeside environment like that of Lake Van, where the breed originated (see page 32).

ABOVE **The Turkish Van cat has adapted to swimming and has a very thick coat. The most favoured Turkish Vans have auburn tails and face markings.**

How old are cats in comparison to human age?

Age-scale comparisons of animals and humans are estimated and based on the known average lifespan of both. It is the speed of the animal's metabolism that is linked to lifespan: some tiny creatures such as shrews are born, mate, reproduce and die within a matter of days, whereas, at the other end of the scale, some large creatures such as elephants and whales take up to a century to complete the same life-to-death processes.

It has always been thought, and indeed many authorities suggest, that each year a cat lives is the equivalent of seven human years. However, this simple process is too crude a calculation and does not take into account the early age at which sexual maturity is reached by cats. A more accurate calculation would be to compare a one-year-old cat to a teenager of about 16, a seven-year-old cat to a middle-aged person of about 40 and a 20-year-old cat to those few people who reach their century. This is summarized in the graph below.

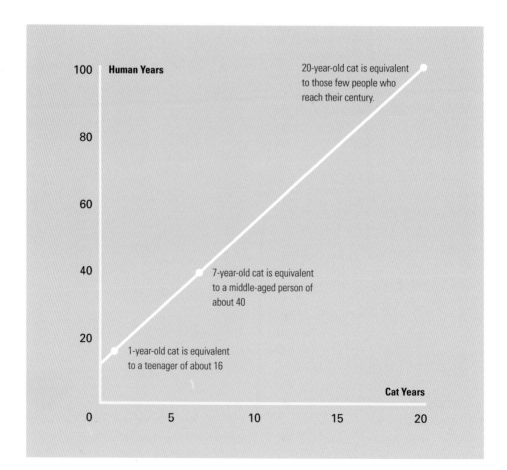

Human Years

- 100 — 20-year-old cat is equivalent to those few people who reach their century.
- 80
- 60
- 40 — 7-year-old cat is equivalent to a middle-aged person of about 40
- 20 — 1-year-old cat is equivalent to a teenager of about 16
- 0

Cat Years

0   5   10   15   20

How long do cats live on average?

The average lifespan of a domesticated cat is somewhere between 12 and 15 years. Of course, some individuals may not reach 12 years while others may survive beyond 20 years. There is little information about longevity in wild cats, but it is thought that the domesticated cat lives twice as long as its feral relative. Needless to say, surviving life in nature is a great deal tougher than leading the cosseted life of a pampered, much-loved house cat. The life-expectancy of a wild cat depends largely upon them finding enough food, avoiding illness and injury and keeping out of the way of predators.

Which is best suited to family life: the pedigree or the 'moggie' cat?

It has long been believed that the unsophisticated cross-bred cat, or moggie, is much tougher and will live longer than the pedigree cat. This is largely based on the fact that, by breeding cats for particular characteristics, we have introduced various medical conditions. There is also a common misconception that pedigree cats are highly strung and naturally neurotic, while moggies are too busy getting on with life to have time to be nervous. The truth is that any kitten that is properly socialized to humans during the litter period will be ideally suited to family life, whether it is a moggie 'free to a good home' or an expensive pedigree cat.

What is a 'working' cat?

Today, a working cat would be found living on a farm, around an industrial site or in a rural home. Here, the presence of rats and mice represents a threat to food stores or structures and wiring, or are a health hazard, and a cat can be used to control them.

The first dynasty of Egyptians has been credited with the earliest use of wild and feral cats to control vermin in grain stores. Later, as they invaded other parts of Europe, the Romans took and

ABOVE The working cat is an instinctive hunter and is employed in many parts of the world to keep rodent populations down.

introduced cats from and to various places to be tamed and used to keep down rats and mice around dwellings and food stores.

The working cat might be shy around humans, but there is no doubting its worth to those who encourage a feline presence to patrol the night-time movements of pests. Cats are masters of hunting and it is known that rats and mice have a genetically inbuilt (innate) fear of them. Vermin will often abandon nest sites where cats are most active.

ABOVE The tabby usually sports a range of patterns. This mackerel or striped tabby is an attractive example of its breed.

What markings make a tabby cat?

The most striking tabby cat has distinctive vertical stripes, known as a 'mackerel' pattern, on its flanks. There are several tabby pattern variations in which the stripes can be replaced by:
• Blotches
• Spots
• Light or dark ticks known as 'agouti'.
The African wild cat, the wild forest cat and the jungle cat all display typical tabby markings.

How should a tortoiseshell cat be marked?

In the most desirable tortoiseshell cats, the dominance of black is infiltrated with a fairly even spread of red and cream. The true tortoiseshell-patterned cat is quite rare and the incredibly high price for a pedigree reflects the rarity of its coloration.

True tortoiseshell-patterned cats are almost all females, as the coloration is linked to the lack of an X chromosome. The few males that carry this beautiful coloration are often sterile, which causes problems for breeders wishing to develop the tortoiseshell cat (see page 85).

ABOVE Tortoiseshell-patterned cats have a mottled coat of red (ginger) and black. They are almost invariably female.

What coloration makes a marmalade cat?

A number of recognized breeds such as the Persian, British shorthair, American short-hair and Siamese carry the marmalade pattern. The pattern is extremely variable and represents a combination of tabby and tortoiseshell-patterned cats. The best marmalade cats display even markings and are usually sturdy males.

Is there really such a thing as a blue cat?

When used to describe cats, the term 'blue' refers to the lovely grey fur that can be found in many pedigree breeds. Representatives include:

- **British Blue short-hair** This breed went into decline following the Second World War, and even today the best and most striking individuals are in a small minority.
- **Long-haired blue** A cross between the Persian and the Angora, this cat came from Iran (formerly Persia).
- **Korat** This is a short-haired blue, with a single coat rather than a double, and

originates from a rare Oriental colour form present in Thailand.

- **Chartreux** This cat is the French equivalent of the British Blue short-hair – to which it is very similar – and is named after the Carthusian monastery with which it was associated. Like the British Blue short-hair, this rare cat is much broader-headed than the Korat. The breed almost became extinct during the 1940s and was re-established by outcrossing the remaining few with the British Blue short-hairs and blue Long-hairs. Records from Thailand (formerly Siam until 1939) and France from seven centuries ago reveal the Korat and the Chartreux to be two of the earliest cats associated with man outside of the ancient Egyptians.

- **Devon Rex** This breed is another British colour version and a relative newcomer, originating in the 1960s (see page 48).

ABOVE A Russian Blue. This breed has a thick shiny coat and emerald green eyes. It is much lighter in build than the British Blue.

What is a colour-point cat?

This term was originally associated with Siamese cats (see page 36). The term colour-point refers to the variation of markings on the face, ears, paws and tail. The colour of these markings are much darker than the main body colour. Breeds include seal, blue, chocolate, lilac (known as frost-point in the USA) red, cream, blue-cream, tortoiseshell-patterned and tabby.

The long-haired colour-point was developed from the Siamese and the Persian/Angora breeds. Careful breeding was used to produce a long-haired cat with the delightful 'point' markings of the Siamese.

What is the Van pattern in cats?

The Van pattern denotes a white-coated cat with solid or tortoiseshell patches on its head and tail. The name is a reference to the Turkish Van cat (see pages 19 and 32), the 'swimming cat' with which it is associated, but the pattern can also be seen in other breeds.

What markings determine a calico cat?

This name is usually used in North America and isn't a breed as such. It is associated with mainly white cats that display varying degrees of tortoiseshell patterning. Even the hint of tortoiseshell markings can define a white cat as a calico.

ABOVE TOP A short-haired Lilac Colour-point. Colour-points have pale bodies and darker markings on the points, the tail, ears, paws and face.

ABOVE A Tortoiseshell (tortie) and White Manx cat. In the USA cats with tortoiseshell and white markings are known as calico cats.

What is a cobby-shaped cat?

The cobby shape is usually associated with the British short-hair, but refers to any cat that is short and small-bodied. With its distinctive round face and robust body, the Persian cat is usually also regarded as cobby in shape.

Why are some cats referred to as wedge-shaped?

This term is almost always associated with Siamese cats. It also applies to other breeds developed from the slender-bodied, narrow-faced, Oriental-type cat.

What is a felinophile?

This is a person who loves cats with a greater passion than most. It is derived from the Latin word for cat lover.

What is ailurophobia?

Someone who hates or fears cats is suffering from ailurophobia. Some famous historical figures were said to be phobic about (or maybe allergic to) cats and are recorded as either fainting or breaking out in a cold sweat whenever a cat appeared. Those believed to have been suffering from ailurophobia, (or elurophobia, felinophobia, galeophobia, gatophobia – all terms apply) include Julius Caesar, Henry II, Emperor Napoleon and Charles XI. At the height of the witchcraft trials, Elizabeth I even burnt cats!

ABOVE TOP This tabby has a typical cobby shape.

ABOVE The faces of Oriental cats are described as narrow or wedge-shaped.

SOME FAMOUS CAT LOVERS

Honoré de Balzac

Brigitte Bardot

Charles Baudelaire

Alexander Borodin

Frances Hodgson Burnett

President George Bush

Karel Capek

Bill Clinton

William Cowper

Dr Erasmus Darwin

W.H. Davies

Thomas Hardy

Victor Hugo

Henry James

Dr Samuel Johnson

Edward Lear

Pope Leo XII

Lenin

Abraham Lincoln

Montaigne

Edgar Allan Poe

Theodore Roosevelt

Christina Rossetti

Saki (H. H. (Hector) Munro)

Sir Walter Scott

Torquato Tasso

Mark Twain (Samuel Langhorne Clemens)

Sir Richard 'Dick' Whittington

William Wordsworth

Breeds

What is the Persian cat?

The Persian cat we know today in all its various colour forms is one of the oldest pedigree breeds around. It also has one of the longest and bushiest coats among the long-haired group of cats. The incredible density of the Persian coat is due to the combination of a large amount of 'down' or fine hair, and long 'guard' hair. This characteristic makes them the softest-coated breed of pet cat. The dense coat also means that Persians are high maintenance, as they require constant grooming to prevent the fur from matting and knotting.

The Victorian Persian, or late 19th-century white-coated cat, was originally crossed with an Angora type to produce the Persian long-haired cat. The earliest European and American forms were white with blue eyes. There were also a number of crosses with blue, cream and black long-haired varieties that produced the orange-eyed form. These two eye-colour forms were characterized

ABOVE LEFT A Persian Seal-point. This long-haired cat with Siamese markings is sometimes known as the Himalayan Persian.

ABOVE A Turkish Angora. This elegant cat takes its name from Angora, the old spelling for Ankara, where it was first bred.

separately just before the Second World War. Persian kittens may display dark markings on the head, but these usually disappear as they mature.

There is a 'Peke-faced' variety of the Persian cat, recognized in the USA, that may still await recognition from breed associations in other countries.

What is the Angora cat?

The original white long-haired cat type was imported to 16th-century France from the capital of Turkey, Ankara (hence Angora). Known from the 19th century, the Angora cat originally displayed a typically finer and less abundant coat than the Persian and was sometimes referred to as a semi-long-haired cat. This type should not be confused with the original European/Turkish form.

The coat of the modern Angora is usually much shorter than that of the Persian, but with many forms and crosses between the two types now available it can be difficult to distinguish them from each other. In addition, from the 1980s Turkish Angoras were imported directly into the USA for breeding and showing.

What is the Birman cat?

This long-haired, blue-eyed cat can trace its origins back to the sacred temple cats of Burma. Despite its supposed mythological link with high priests, the Birman probably shares its ancestry with other Oriental cats such as the seal-point Siamese. It is distinguished from the Siamese by its white paws and longer coat. There are about ten colour-point types (see page 24) including seal, chocolate, blue, tabby, cream and lilac, and a single female colour form known as seal-tortoiseshell point.

What characteristics identify a Chinchilla cat?

The Chinchilla cat is an Angora/Persian cross introduced to Britain in the late 19th century. In the USA, this breed conforms to the standards given for the Persian breed in general; in Britain, the specific standard allows for a more finely boned cat.

ABOVE TOP A Chinchilla is an Angora–Persian cross.

ABOVE The Birman was introduced to Europe in the 1920s when it was known as the Sacred Cat of Burma.

What is the Cymric cat?

Named after the Welsh word for Wales (Cymru), this is a rare long-haired type of Manx cat. It is therefore characterized by its tail stump plus longer coat. There are some lovely colour forms, including orange-eyed white and reds, with three different tail-forms – 'rumpy' (almost no tail), 'stumpy' (very short tail) and 'longy' (extended stumpy tail). The Cymric (pronounced 'kumrik') has strong support in the USA.

What is the Turkish Van cat?

This long-haired Angora-type cat originated from the Lake Van region of Turkey. It is a lively, white-coated cat with auburn-marked ears or face. The Turkish Van has a long history of enjoying water, being bathed and swimming (see page 19) – almost like the feline equivalent of the otter. Although known to the local Turkish people for hundreds of years, the breed is relatively new to countries outside Eastern Europe. It was introduced to Britain in the 1950s and to the USA in the 1980s. Deafness is common among blue-eyed Turkish Vans.

What is the Maine Coon cat?

This tough and hardy cat was the first long-haired breed to originate in the USA. It is a very distinctive and relatively large breed, with 'fat cat' males growing to 8 kg (10 lb). The Coon part of the name alludes to its distinctive racoon-like brush tail. There are historical references that suggest the origins of the Maine Coon lie in the 18th-century French court with Mary Antoinette, who is thought to have exported them to avoid their persecution during the Revolution.

What is the Norwegian Forest cat?

This is one of the newest discoveries in the world of fancy cat breeds. The Norwegian Forest cat has a distinctive 'double' coat that is water resistant –

perfectly suited to the woodland and rock outcrop feral lifestyle its name suggests. In appearance, it is very similar to the Maine Coon (see left). The Norwegian Forest cat has the distinction of being fabled in Norse legends as a 'fairy cat', and in its homeland it is known as *Norsk skaukatt* (sky cat), being famed for its incredible climbing abilities.

What is the Siberian Forest cat?

It has been debated over whether this ancient breed, which can be traced back over more than a thousand years, is the forerunner of all long-haired cat breeds, including Persians and Angoras. This is a rough-and-ready breed, genetically traceable to modern-day tabby cats that live around St Petersburg, and has an extremely thick coat to help it survive the extremes of a Siberian climate. Relatively scarce outside its Russian homeland, this breed is distinctively tabby, with its colouring bias perhaps due to wild or feral matings.

FAR LEFT The Cymric is a rare form of Manx cat.

LEFT Norwegian Forest cats are one of the newest breeds. They have a double water-resistant coat.

ABOVE RIGHT The Turkish Van cat is famed for its swimming ability.

RIGHT Chocolate Point is a popular colouring for Ragdolls, an American breed which is particularly docile and relaxed.

What is the Ragdoll cat?

The earliest record of the Ragdoll is open to some speculation, because it was said to have originated from a mis-mated Californian Persian queen. The supposed charm of the blue-eyed Ragdoll is that it naturally becomes limp when handled.

This characteristic has mythically been attributed to the litter mother giving birth after suffering a broken pelvis in a road traffic accident. There are three basic coat patterns in the Ragdoll – bicolor (white plus another colour), colour-point and mitted (mitten-like white front feet) – with colour types including seal, blue, chocolate and lilac.

What is the Somali cat?

This breed originated from longer-haired kittens from Abyssinian cat litters. It has a vibrant coat that shimmers due to each individual hair having multiple bands of colour. Named after the Somali African state adjacent to Ethiopia (formerly known as Abyssinia), the name indicates the association with the Abyssinian cat: the Somali cat is characterized as a medium- to long-haired form of the short-haired Abyssinian. This breed may actually share its roots with the Abyssinian, one of the oldest of all domesticated cats, originating from an ancient breed that now has many influences around the world.

What is the Tiffanie cat?

This breed represents the long-haired form of the Burmese or Asian cat (see pages 42 and 43) and is the only long-haired member of the Asian group. Traditionally it is dark brown, but tabby, blue and lilac colour forms are also seen. The Tiffanie originated from an accidental mating between a long-haired Chinchilla (see page 31) and a lilac Burmese.

ABOVE TOP A Blue Somali. Somalis are a long-haired version of the Abyssinian and have a gentle nature and quiet voice.

ABOVE The rare Chocolate Silken-tipped Tiffanie. Tiffanies are affectionate cats and have a loud voice when they want attention.

What is the Javanese cat?

This is a long-haired Oriental breed, named after the Far Eastern island of Java. It looks like a cross between a Siamese and a broad-tailed Maine Coon type (see page 32). In Britain, the name Javanese is attributed to kittens that originated from a breeding programme aimed at recovering the Angora breed. In North America the name tends to be associated with Balinese cats (see below) that do not conform to the four traditional Siamese colour-points.

What is the Balinese cat?

The name Balinese, from the island of Bali, was first given to longer-haired kittens of Siamese cats. The long-haired gene probably has its origins in Angoras, which were occasionally mated with Siamese colour-points.

BELOW A Balinese cat. These long-haired Siamese are named after the island in Indonesia. They were first recognized by American cat societies in the 1960s and in Britain ten years later.

BELOW BOTTOM A Javanese Chocolate Tortoiseshell, a breed named after the Indonesian island.

What is the Scottish Fold cat?

The first Scottish Fold, recorded in 1951, was a short-haired cat, as was one of her kittens. However, the breeding programme that resulted from this produced long-haired kittens. This breed is characterized by its thick coat and a deformity that causes the distinctive folded or flap-backed ears. The kittens are actually born with straight ears but these start to fold when they are about three weeks old. Scottish Fold cats are reputed to have a gentle disposition.

What is the American Curl cat?

This breed originated from a Californian breeder who adopted two kittens and noticed that the ear cartilage on one curled back. The first litter from this cat produced four kittens with the same ear deformity, and these individuals later helped to establish the breed from the early 1980s. There is a variety of colour forms, from black through to mackerel tabby. The American Curl is now established in both long- and short-haired types.

Did the Siamese cat originate from Thailand (formerly Siam)?

Yes, the Siamese cat probably did come from the Far East, and gets its Oriental name-tag from that background. Originating in the 16th century or even earlier, these cats were held in such high esteem in the court of Siam that stealing a royal cat was once punishable by death.

The wild form probably inhabited the tropical rainforests of Thailand and Indonesia.

The Siamese is a delicately slender, long-legged cat known for its very distinctive body shape, ear outline and colour-point coat pattern, although European and North American breed standards on these points vary slightly. This extremely popular breed has four classic colour-point variations: seal, blue, chocolate and lilac (see page 24). These have been further developed into additional colour types. In the USA, cross-breeding with other cats has produced new colours and patterns known as 'colour-point short-hairs'. Generations on from early experimental colour-points, these cats have been crossed back with pure Siamese to create a stronger bloodline that is closer to the original.

What is the British short-hair cat?

This cobby-shaped (see page 26) cat's ancestors were first brought to Britain over 2,000 years ago by the invading Romans. A strong, muscular, short-legged cat, this is one of the stockiest breeds of domesticated cat. The American form of the British short-hair, first taken on board ships by the Pilgrim Fathers to keep down vermin, has developed slightly differently: it is more elongated and lean in body shape, and slightly longer in the leg than its British counterpart.

The British short-hair is one of the most popular cats in Britain, although in recent decades it has been somewhat overshadowed by the Persian, Siamese

ABOVE **A Siamese Blue Point. Blue points were first recognized in the late 19th century.**

RIGHT **A typical British Short-hair, with the chunky, cobby build and short, sturdy legs of this popular cat.**

and Exotic breeds. It still comes in a wonderful array of colour types, from all-white through cream, blue-grey, silver, brown, red, mackerel tabby, tortoiseshell, spotted and bicolor, to smoke and black.

Breed standards for the pedigree British short-hair were only introduced in the 1980s, but the pedigree cat is fast becoming established. For show purposes, the eyes of the pedigree cat should be extremely colour-defined, with a distinct amber-iris characteristic. The popular colour forms for pedigree cats are all-black, classic or mackerel tabby, and self-red.

What is the Exotic cat?

This breed is basically a short-haired Persian, probably developed for owners with an allergy to long-haired cats (see pages 54 and 60). There are parallel colour forms to the Persian and, because of the advantages over long-haired breeds, the popularity of the Exotic has grown over the past few decades.

What is the Manx cat?

This cat probably shares its heritage with Celtic descendants of the Scottish wild cat. Although there is much local Isle of Man mythology connected to this distinctive tail-less or stumpy-tailed cat (one story suggests that it originated from a sinking Spanish Galleon, another that the tail was taken by fairies), it is the isolation of the mutant gene in an island environment that has sustained the breed for many centuries. There is a

ABOVE LEFT A Blue Exotic Short Hair, a breed developed for owners with allergies to their pets.

ABOVE A Manx cat. These short-haired cats from the Isle of Man are known as Rumpies, Rumpy-risers, Stumpies or Longies according to the conformation of their tails.

lethal gene-pairing that can result from a rumpy $\times$ rumpy mating which produces kitten fatalities.

What is the American short-hair cat?

This is the North American form of the British short-haired cat that first made its way to America on ships that carried the Pilgrim Fathers. These cats were prized for their finely tuned rodent-hunting skills, and were included on the ships to keep down rat populations and protect grain and fresh food stores. The breed quickly became established in the early settlements and over the centuries has deviated only marginally in shape and colour forms from its British ancestors (see page 37).

What is the American Wirehair cat?

The origins of the American Wirehair cat can be attributed to a striking red-and-white kitten that came from a farm in New York State. This breed has an unusual coat in that each hair is thinner than usual and is bent or crimped, hence

the reference to 'wire' in its name. Rarely encountered outside the USA, this breed is not dissimilar to the distinctive British Cornish Rex (see page 47). An American Wirehair cat with curly whiskers is highly prized in its homeland.

What is the European short-hair cat?

The distinction between the European and the British short-hair is minimal, with the two breeds overlapping. They share common ancestry in that the populations both resulted from the spread of the Roman Empire. The European is less cobby-shaped (see page 26) than the British breed with a slightly longer, slimmer face and perhaps more elegant overall look. It tends to be calm and affectionate by nature.

What is the Chartreux cat?

This is an extremely ancient French short-haired breed. It tends to be very laidback in temperament and, while not aggressive, is a good hunter. It was developed by 14th-century Carthusian monks and should not be confused with the more round-faced British Blue cat (see page 23). Visually difficult to distinguish from its British look-alike, the Chartreux has a marginally lighter coat. Legend suggests that Crusaders returned from the Holy Land with these cats, and the monks are said to have controlled access to the breed by releasing only neutered individuals.

ABOVE **The Chartreux, an ancient French breed, can be difficult to distinguish from the British Blue. They share a similar colour and build.**

What is the Bengal cat?

This breed was developed by an American geneticist who cross-mated a male domestic cat with a female Asian leopard cat. The resulting breed, one of the most striking spotted-patterned of all cats with a distinctively thick coat, is said to have the look of a wild cat with the temperament of a domesticated one. Bengals are known to enjoy playing with water – an indication of their natural jungle cat ancestry.

What is the Japanese Bobtail cat?

This predominantly white-coated breed is a stump-tailed cat. Known in Japan as Mi-Ke (meaning three-furred), the Japanese Bobtail is popular as a good luck symbol and is thought to have been taken to that country from the Chinese mainland over 1,000 years ago.

What is the Russian cat?

The first short-haired 'blue' cats came from Russia, where they were referred to as Archangel Blues. This name has

ABOVE The Bengal is prized for its leopard ancestry. Bengals which may be marbled or spotted have short, thick coats with a lustrous sheen.

LEFT A Russian Blue. These cats are sometimes known as Archangel cats, after the White Sea port through which they first reached western Europe.

ABOVE The Korat, from Thailand, is prized in its homeland for its potential to bring its owner good luck. Its blue fur has silver tips.

its origins in that of a Russian port, from which sailors are thought to have set sail as they exported the cats to Europe. Russian blues have a dense, seal-like fur that would probably enable them to survive the extremes of a Siberian winter.

What is the Korat cat?

Another distinctive blue short-haired breed, the Korat originated in Thailand. It is similar in looks to the Russian Shorthair except it has a single coat rather than a double and its eyes are a different shade of green. This feline beauty is much prized as a rarity in its homeland and, although it has a rather innocent expression, it is a rather strong-willed breed that likes to get its own way.

What is the Burmese cat?

The Burmese cat originated from a mating between a red tabby and a breed with an Oriental/Thai background. The Burmese combines the eyes and slender, fine-boned qualities of a Siamese with a satin-soft coat. It includes the typical Siamese range of colours, from cream through chocolate to tortoiseshell.

What is the Burmilla cat?

ABOVE TOP A Cream Burmese. Burmese are lively, affectionate cats with good health and a reputation for living long lives.

ABOVE The Burmilla resulted from an accidental mating between a Chinchilla and a Burmese. The breed was officially recognized in 1990.

First recognized in the 1980s, this breed resulted from a cross between Burmese and long-haired Chinchilla cats. With white, silver and light-cream colour types, this pretty, sociable breed clearly reveals it origins.

What is the Asian Brown Mackerel Tabby cat?

Like the Burmilla, this breed was first recognized in the 1980s and resulted from an identical cross between the Burmese and long-haired Chinchilla. The Asian Brown Mackerel Tabby cat, less Oriental in character than its cousins, is quite a distinctive type, although there are also other less markedly patterned types that are not as striking.

What is the Bombay cat?

This coal-coloured breed originated in a 1950s mating between a sable Burmese and a black American short-haired cat. This imaginative cross produced an Oriental-looking, miniature panther-like cat. It has deep copper-coloured eyes which sometimes fade or turn slightly green as the cat gets older. The Bombay is often put into the Asian group and, although established as a breed in 1976, is still not widely recognized.

It's beautiful sleek black coat is very easy to maintain, needing only a quick rubdown with a chamois leather in order to maintain the sheen.

ABOVE **The Singapura originated from the feral street cats of Singapore and was developed in the USA in the 1970s.**

LEFT **The Abyssinian cat is believed to be one of the oldest breeds of all, with a conformation similar to that of ancient Egyptian cats.**

What is the Singapura cat?

This breed, once known only as a street or feral cat, has a very recent history in domestication. Records show that it was taken from the island of Singapore (Malayan name: Singapura) in the 1970s and early 1980s by an American enthusiast. A delightful sable-coloured, silky-coated, small Oriental cat, the breed is said to be extremely instinctive. This must be due mainly to its recent feral background and means that this rare breed is not entirely suited to owners who want a calm and undemanding cat.

What is the Abyssinian cat?

This is one of the oldest of all domesticated cat breeds. It was first established in Britain in 1868 by soldiers returning from war in Abyssinia (now Ethiopia) and was accepted as a breed in 1882. It is similar in appearance to cats illustrated in tombs and mummified individuals that can be dated to ancient Egyptian dynasties. The common forms are red to biscuit-brown, the perfect camouflage in its natural North African habitat. Its coat pattern is the result of a gene which makes each hair striped dark and light bands. The Abyssinian is an athletic, inquisitive creature and is also known to be almost silent.

Short-haired breeds **45**

What is the Ocicat cat?

Developed from a cross between a male chocolate-point Siamese and a female Abyssinian × seal-point Siamese, the American Ocicat has superb markings. The spotted, almost ocelot-like wild cat appearance of the most common tabby-like form, and chocolate and silver colours, appeal to most cat lovers.

What is the California Spangled cat?

This very recent breed was developed from a number of others. These are said to include a spotted Manx, silver-spotted tabby long-hair, seal-point Siamese, British and American short-hairs, feral cats from Cairo, and Asian non-pedigrees. The new breed arrived in the USA to a fanfare. The Holy Grail of producing the strikingly spot-patterned, wild-looking cats – almost achieved with the development of the Ocicat – was finally located when the California Spangled cat was successfully produced and offered to Americans as one of the most expensive designer cats available. The extraordinary price for these naturally marked kittens was deliberately fixed at an artificially high level, because the breed was developed to help create funding for use in highlighting the plight of large wild cats in nature.

BELOW **The short-haired Ocicat is prized for its ocelot-like markings.**

ABOVE Snowshoe cats from the USA display distinctive white paws. They are sometimes known as Silver Laces.

ABOVE The curly coat of the Cornish Rex has an unusual appearance. All colours and patterns are permissible in this breed.

What is the Snowshoe cat?

This distinctively white-footed cat was developed in the USA in the 1960s. It arose from a series of crosses between Siamese cats and American short-hairs and is rarely found outside North America. There are two different patterns of Snowshoe cat: the mitted, which has little white, and the bi-colour which has more white on the body and face. Purists among Siamese breeders often express concern that the 'snowshoe' markings will cross over into the much older breed via indiscriminate mating.

This breed are very affectionate with quiet voices, but, surprisingly, they can also be very talkative.

What is the Cornish Rex cat?

This woolly-looking, short-haired cat first appeared in the 1950s when a British farm cat produced one curly-haired male kitten in her litter. It was consequently bred back with her. Since then, this breed has been crossed with Burmese and British Shorthairs. Its short coat is incredibly soft to the touch, resembling velvet, and is said to benefit from an occasional 'bran bath' (see page 107). It is not suited to cold and wet conditions, which means this breed is a good candidate for keeping as an indoor house cat. There are a number of colour types including white, cream, silver, smoke, chocolate and tortoiseshell.

LEFT The Devon Rex came about from a gene mutation. It was first recognized in Britain in 1967 and in the USA in 1979.

What is the Sphynx cat?

This apparently hairless cat, often found without whiskers, is the product of a natural mutation first recorded in 1966. However, the Sphynx cat probably has a gene history going back centuries, with obscure references made to it around the world.

Some cat fancy associations choose to take a negative view of this suede-like, downy-haired breed, but it does have its champions. Cat lovers with hair allergies are often drawn to the Sphynx, which can provoke horrified looks from those who lack an affinity with felines.

What is the Devon Rex cat?

The product of a different gene mutation, this curly-coated cat appeared about ten years after its Cornish cousin. It is said to have resulted from a cross between a curled-coated feral male and a stray British straight-haired female. The gene for a curly coat is recessive and inbreeding became necessary in order to continue the breed. The slightly 'clownish' look of this cat is matched by its clumsy and amusing outlook on life.

A new American breed, known as the Poodle, has been developed from cross-matings between Devon Rex and Scottish Fold cats (see page 36). This combines the curly coat with the folded ears, to produce a rather comical-looking cat.

What is the Selkirk Rex cat?

Records suggest that this very young breed, recognized in 1987, resulted from a curly-coated female stray mated with a black Persian. There are long- and short-haired types, with males more readily obtained because females are usually restricted to breeders who wish to retain them for their programmes. This cat's distinctive patches of curls, rather than a uniform curly coat, make it unusual among Rex types. The patches of curls, although apparent at birth, disappear shortly afterwards. They reappear when the cat is around eight to ten months old and stay for the duration of their life.

ABOVE The Sphynx is sometimes called the hairless cat, but it is actually one of the shortest haired of all cat breeds.

RIGHT An Oriental Short-Hair. These cats share the Siamese build but have a wide range of coat markings without the distinctive Siamese pattern.

What is the Oriental cat?

This clearly Siamese-looking breed came about as a result of various test crosses between other short-haired breeds. Cat associations and breeders brought all these experimental crosses into a general group known as Orientals. A distinctive form was developed from a Siamese/Russian Blue cross to create the Oriental Ebony.

What is the Tonkinese cat?

The Tonkinese resulted from a cross made between a Burmese and a Siamese cat in the 1930s. Kittens are said to represent both breeds – they are sometimes referred to as the Golden Siamese because of the Burmese colour influence. It was 40 years before this breed was recognized by breed associations around the world.

BELOW Tonkinese, which have both Siamese and Burmese characteristics, have a reputation as friendly, lively cats.

What is the Havana Brown cat?

The Havana Brown colour form was developed from the Oriental group of cats. Known in Britain as the Chestnut Brown Foreign, early Havana Brown cats came from a chocolate-point Siamese mated with a black non-pedigree. It has bright green eyes and a beautiful chocolate-brown coat. They are very physical cats and good climbers with their oval, compact paws, despite their graceful appearance. They are known to be very sweet, sociable and highly intelligent.

What is the Egyptian Mau cat?

The origins of this naturally spotted, Siamese-like cat are likely to lie with the African wild cat. The first recognized Egyptian Mau was brought to the USA by a Russian princess in 1956 and recorded as being the result of crosses between undetermined European short-haired cats. The Egyptian Mau has a cobby shape like the American short-hair, combined with the Oriental sleekness of body with a fine, silky coat. The ideal coloration was developed to be as similar as possible to that of the cats that appeared in ancient Egyptian wall paintings. In Britain, this breed is known as the Oriental Spotted Tabby. It is a highly intelligent breed and very loyal. They are known to have soft melodious voices.

ABOVE The appearance of Oriental cats clearly reveals their Siamese ancestry. The Havana Brown has a smooth, lustrous coat and vivid green eyes.

A Cat of Your Own

Should I get a male or a female cat?

Once neutered, either a male or a female cat can make an ideal companion animal. Some owners have a preference often based on their previous relationships with cats. Sometimes elderly people express a desire for a cat that is the opposite gender to them, to create a 'replacement partner'.

Adult entire (un-neutered) cats are less straightforward as house cats.
Males (toms) will:
- 'Mark' their territory by spraying urine, both outside and inside the house, in order to attract females.
- Be more likely to expand their territory in order to seek out a female.

Females (queens) will:
- Come into 'season', ready to conceive, once or twice a year and often be extremely restless, even agitated, throughout the day and night.
- Issue long, loud caterwauling noises when in season in order to attract or maintain contact with interested male cats.

A responsible cat owner will wish to avoid unplanned pregnancies, even in other people's cats, and will have their cat neutered when it reaches sexual maturity. Once neutered, a house cat will often become more attached to its owner and may show a reduced desire to roam great distances from the home. However, neutering does not prevent spraying or aggressive behaviour in cats (see page 196).

A kitten should be considered for neutering at around 6 months of age. The cost is different for males and females, since spaying a queen involves more complex surgery. If you acquire an adult cat from a rescue centre it will most likely already have been neutered. However, this is not a legal requirement so do check with the centre first.

Should I go for a kitten or an adult cat?

There are pros and cons for both. Kittens are usually cute and appealing animals, but they do require a great deal of commitment in their early months. At 6 months old, maturing cats do not require quite the same level of attention as young kittens. Cats become fully mature at about 1 year old, although it has been said that cats love to play and never actually grow up – they just grow larger! The table (right) lists the pros and cons of acquiring a kitten or an adult cat.

Is a short-haired cat easier to maintain than a long-haired breed?

Long-haired cats require extensive grooming on a daily basis if their coats are not to become matted and difficult to clean. As a minimum, they will need about 20 minutes of grooming at least three times a week in order for their coats to remain knot-free and in good condition. If you cannot guarantee to provide this amount of brushing or combing attention, choose a short-haired variety.

People who suffer from dust and hair allergies are often adversely affected by a long-haired cat. Those who are allergic to

CAT OR KITTEN?

	Pros	Cons
Kitten	Very adaptable. Easier to socialize with humans. Easier to socialize with other house pets. More likely to socialize with an existing adult cat. Offers the fun of seeing its development from kitten to adult. Easy to house train at an early age.	May not house train immediately. Needs more interactive attention than an adult cat. Needs regular feeds and ideally should not be left alone for long periods. Not always adaptable to home and handling changes.
Adult Cat	Usually house trained. Already socialized. Does not need constant interaction. Can be fed once a day.	May be difficult to socialize with humans with whom it is not familiar. More difficult to socialize with other house pets. Usually very difficult to socialize with an existing adult cat. Does not offer the fun of seeing its development from kitten to adult.

ABOVE **Short-haired cats are a more sensible choice than the long-haired breeds for cat owners with allergies.**

cats are usually severely allergic to long-haired types, whereas short-haired cats tend to affect people who are extremely allergic to cat hairs (see also page 60).

Is there a hairless breed of cat?

Although not truly hairless, the Sphynx cat has only the slightest down hair that appears more like a skin (see page 48). This black or brown-and-white cat originated from a breeder in Ontario, Canada, after a hairless individual was discovered with a litter of kittens. It is

said that hairless cats had been recorded in France and Mexico before the Sphynx was discovered, but these aberrant individuals were not developed for a breeding line.

Are there large and small breeds from which to choose?

Cat breeds do not really vary greatly in adult size in the way that dog breeds do. However, a diminutive, short-haired cat would appear miniature alongside an overweight, chunky-bodied, long-haired Persian cat, for example. Lengthy fur and a muscular body considerably increase the outline shape of a cat.

Where should I obtain my kitten or cat?

Professional breeders are listed in breed registers or at your local veterinary surgery. You can also find their names through the advertisements in leading cat magazines and on the internet.

Looking through books about cat breeds will give you an idea about which types appeal to you, but attending cat shows to see them first-hand is even better. You will also be able to see the top show cats and form an opinion on the quality of a particular breeder's animals.

Your veterinary surgeon will probably have local knowledge of cat breeders and be aware of those with good standards and an interest in the long-term well-being of the kittens they offer to members of the public. Professional

ABOVE **The Sphynx is not truly hairless but has the shortest coat of all breeds. The breed obtained Championship status in 1971.**

breeders with the highest standards will usually provide healthy kittens – recommendation is often the best route. Keep your budget in mind: prices will be highest for the most sought-after breeds and the offspring of show winners.

Are there places to avoid when I'm looking to acquire a kitten?

There are several less satisfactory sources for kittens.

- Kittens on offer in a pet shop or large store are usually the result of an unplanned mating. The owner of the litter mother may have sold them simply to avoid the cost and work of arranging to home them all.

- The source of pet-shop kittens may be particularly dubious if the owner has little interest in the welfare of their breeding cats and regards them simply as a source of income.

- Kittens from farms or that are the result of an accidental mating may have a feral cat in their bloodline, and this may predispose the kitten towards developing behavioural problems in adulthood.

- The same can apply to kittens offered 'free to a good home' in newspapers, on notice boards and from home breeders.

You need to be aware of these factors but it doesn't mean that a happy and healthy kitten cannot come from these sources.

ABOVE It can be a good idea to choose a cat from a rescue centre, but many abandoned cats and kittens are nervous or afraid.

Can I import a cat from another country?

The laws on importing cats vary between countries. Most have strict quarantine regulations, the length of which depends on the likelihood of endemic animals being known carriers of rabies and other exotic diseases. Cats that have been microchipped, vaccinated and subjected to veterinary checks can be moved more easily between countries that have created new pet importation rules. Some countries have set up schemes whereby, if an animal complies with all the rules of the scheme, they can avoid spending six months in quarantine. Check with a veterinary practice about the current requirements well in advance of intended travel.

How do I adopt a cat?

Rescue centres will generally have a range of abandoned kittens and cats in need of caring homes. These may include moggies, pet-quality kittens and sometimes pedigree cats. Such centres will be listed in local newspapers or telephone books.

Non-pedigree cats are often advertised in local newspapers. They are always much cheaper than pedigree cats and may even be offered 'free to a good home'.

What should we do if a cat adopts us?

It is not unusual for cats to locate potential new homes. They use their instincts to detect 'cat-friendly' humans – offering food is a good sign – and will home in on a person with a charitable disposition.

If a cat adopts you, there are various steps you can take:

- Check to see if it is wearing a collar with a name and address tag.
- Check with the local police and rescue centre to see if the cat has been reported missing.
- Place an advertisement in the local paper describing it (many papers offer a free placement in the 'lost and found' section).
- Check with neighbours to establish if anyone has lost a cat that fits the description of the one that has placed itself on your doorstep.

It is also worth looking through local newspapers and scanning notice boards in local stores, for example – you may discover that the cat already has a good home and owners who are worried about it and desperate for its safe return.

If the cat stays with you for a week or more, it is a good idea for your vet to carry out a health check and give any necessary precautionary vaccinations.

If another cat is already resident in your home, it is wise to avoid taking in a strange one as this is often the trigger for the existing cat to leave.

We have found a stray cat – what should we do if we want to keep it?

First, you should make any necessary checks to establish that the cat who has decided to move in with you really is 'detached' from its owners (see left). Then, there is little else to do but take care of your new feline family member.

There are many reasons as to why cats become detached from their owners. For example, a cat may be left behind when a family moves home, or a cat refuses to leave its territory even though the owners have. My first family cat was acquired in just this way: when I discussed the situation with my new neighbours, I discovered that the owners who had moved away owned a large number of cats and probably didn't consider the lovely black British short-hair left behind to be one of the close members of the family. Their loss was certainly my gain.

Is it true that some people can be phobic towards cats?

Known variously as ailurophobia, elurophobia, felinophobia, galeophobia or gatophobia, a fear of cats is very real for some people. Phobias develop from trauma or by negative association. It is believed, for example, that a sleeping infant who has been startled by a cat which has curled up close by and begun to purr loudly may develop such a phobia. In some instances, a cat-phobic individual may have been frightened by an aggressive cat in real life, in cartoons, or in television and film images, and a fear association then progresses into adulthood. However, to put cat phobia into perspective: for every human who is frightened of cats there are a hundred thousand who just adore them!

How will I know if I (or any other member of my family) has a cat allergy?

Make sure that any family member with a suspected allergy encounters cats prior to introducing one into your home. This is to establish whether or not there are any family members who are allergic to either cat hair or dead skin dust. Each person should pass a 'handling test', by allowing them to stroke a cat to ascertain if an allergic reaction is triggered, before a cat is brought into the home long term.

Short-haired cats, especially the black and black-and-white varieties, are probably the most popular non-pedigree types available. It is these you are likely to choose from if your budget doesn't allow for a pedigree cat, so any test for potential cat allergies should be undertaken with these types.

BELOW Some people quickly discover that they are allergic to cats. This is best established in advance.

Is it true that people are more likely to be allergic to dark-haired than light-haired cats?

The colour of a cat's coat is thought to have an effect on individuals who may be allergic to them. One research study showed that whether a cats was kept in or out of the bedroom proved not to influence the allergic reaction in their owners. But, perhaps rather surprisingly, those people keeping a dark-haired cat were 75 percent more likely to display allergic symptoms than those with a light-haired cat. Although the real reason for this discrepancy is currently unknown, it is probably related to the thickness or composition of the hairs.

Are rescue cats more prone to health and behaviour problems?

Cats and kittens that are up for adoption often have an unknown past. This means that they could have suffered abuse or experienced a dysfunctional or feral background. Sometimes cats have been considered abandoned or lost and have simply been handed in at a rescue centre. Cats in both categories can be more vulnerable but, conversely, they can also be tough and more adaptable than the cat that has led a comfortable life.

There is always an element of luck in obtaining a rescue cat as often you only have your instinct to go by. However, the rewards can be great: you may gain a feline friend that enriches the lives of all who encounter it.

What will a rescue centre expect of us if we want to adopt a cat?

Most rescue centres will follow a similar procedure with prospective adoptive families. They will:
- Take down basic details about you, your family and your home.
- Ascertain whether or not you have had experience of owning a cat.
- Ask if you want a kitten or an adult cat.
- Decide if you will make a suitable owner.
- Try to match you up with the ideal cat.

BELOW Dark-haired cats are more likely to trigger an allergic reaction than light-coloured cats.

LEFT Owners are more likely to encounter behaviour problems when keeping two cats rather than one.

RIGHT Choosing an adult cat can offer advantages over picking a kitten, however eye-catching, provided it is socialized.

Is it best to get two kittens so they won't be lonely?

Research suggests that you are far more likely to encounter behavioural problems with two cats than with one or a group. Adult cats naturally compete with each other, although a satisfactory socialization can be achieved if cats are exposed to each other from the early kitten stage.

At what age is it safe to allow a kitten outside my home?

The ideal time is when a kitten has reached about 24 weeks, is fully vaccinated and neutered, is settled with you and has established a mental map of home. It can then be allowed to begin expanding its horizons: the yard or garden would be the next step, with several brief daily sessions where the kitten is allowed to walk about and explore the immediate surrounding home boundary.

The personality of the kitten will dictate how fast and how far the explorations progress. Kittens are driven by curiosity, and the extrovert will soon, be exploring its surroundings, have its head in the watering can or under the shed and be expanding its new territory into the flower beds. The quieter individual will wait for its owner, as 'lead cat', to make the steps forward and show it the way.

How will a kitten know its way back to my home?

Kittens and cats immediately begin to develop a mental territory map, as they begin to expand their explorations beyond the home boundaries. They also leave fresh scent marks with urine, faeces and from the scent glands on their head and paws. It would be rare for a kitten to brave a great distance from a known territory. However, explorations can become a feline adventure when an interesting fence, wall or group of trees is encountered.

The excitement and fear is also heightened when another cat appears. If the other cat begins a chase, in an effort to drive away a potential competitor, the kitten can quickly become territorially disorientated. If the kitten is chased back home, the experience is just part of a

learning curve; if chased away from familiar territory, the consequences can be much more serious. With this in mind, it is always wise to supervise the early outdoor explorations of a young cat and keep in contact with it by using food treats, interaction and affection to keep it safe and close to home.

Is it possible for me to keep an indoor cat, as I live in a high-rise apartment?

An indoor cat would be entirely suitable for life in a high-rise building. Nevertheless, balconies and terraces may have to be 'out of bounds' and secure because of the danger of accidental falls.

It is possible to control the 'ins and outs' of an outdoor cat by physically taking it to ground level and then carrying it inside again when you are ready, but this would suit only the most dedicated of cat owners.

How do I choose the right kitten?

There is an element of luck involved in selecting a kitten to be the calm and loving pet you desire. Professional breeders can introduce you to the litter mother and illustrate her best points. If she has a good temperament, and the litter has been properly cared for and not

BELOW Choosing the perfect kitten from a delightful litter like this one is an extremely difficult task, but sometimes a kitten will choose you.

RIGHT Cat activity centres offer a selection of games and pastimes. They are particularly suitable for housebound cats.

removed from her too soon, then the kittens should be fine. However, even someone with an animal behaviour background can only take a snapshot observation of a litter of kittens and hope to make a correct decision.

There is one simple method to select a kitten: simply hold out your hand and the kitten may choose you!

How do I choose the right adult cat?

If choosing an adult cat to adopt, it would be useful to visit and offer some physical contact. Once you, as the prospective owner, have been 'accepted' by the cat, the adoption procedure can go ahead.

In home situations, this would be a realistic strategy to adopt in order to avoid taking on a nervous or aggressive cat. In rescue centres, it is not usually possible to make valid personality assessments, because cats rarely show true behaviours (beyond aggression and timidity) when they are maintained in temporary accommodation. It may be possible for a member of the centre to offer a generalized assessment to confirm the cat's sociability. If it can be stroked and picked up without fear or aggression, this will provide an indicator.

Nervous cats look for bolt holes in the smallest places and they should not be

SEEK OUT THE AVERAGE

The general advice to 'seek out the average individual' when choosing a kitten is not altogether realistic. To attempt to do this, you need to time your visit to coincide with activity from the kittens – the breeder may be able to predict the active times and suggest an optimum visit time for you. The most realistic approach would then be to choose an 'average' kitten in the form of its activity and personality. To make a truly accurate decision, you would need to spend days to gain an insight beyond those obvious behaviours that occur at 'sleep' time and 'activity' time.

LEFT A cat flap allows a pet freedom to come and go at any time of the day or night, and saves the owner from continually opening and shutting doors.

Should I install a cat flap?

Cat flaps are almost mandatory for outgoing, outdoor cats. They allow free entry and exit for the home cat with an exploring personality. One downside of the open-door facility a cat flap provides is that other cats from the neighbourhood can utilize it to gain access to your home. This can trigger behavioural problems in some nervous cats, for whom trespassing is the feline equivalent of house burglary.

What type of cat flap is best?

Most pet behaviourists would advise the use of controlled-entry cat flaps. These are magnetized cat flaps where a collar on the cat triggers the flap to open. The positive aspect of these flaps is that they are ideal for owners with outdoor cats that need to get in and out of the home at various times of the day and night, particularly if the owners aren't at home very much. However, there is some evidence to suggest that if a cat is being chased by another cat when entering the flap while wearing a magnetized collar, it offers its pursuer an opportunity to follow through at the same time, which could be terrifying for your poor cat!

Also available are cat flaps with locking devices that allow you to keep your cat in when you want.

judged simply on a need to find sanctuary from a 'hostile' world. Such cats may stabilize in a caring home and eventually show a sociable personality. Prolonged observation and contact on more than one occasion would provide a realistic assessment of personality.

If my cat wanders away from my home, how far can I expect it to go?

This will depend on several factors, including the cat's gender and the density of the local cat population.

- A neutered cat will rarely stray beyond the local houses and streets.
- Entire cats, especially toms, may have a territorial range that extends up to 20 times larger than that of the contented house cat.

- In urban areas, where cat populations are most dense, a wandering or exploring cat may remain within a few streets. In this situation, the cat's behaviour will be dominated by positioning itself to watch the world go by and watching for potential prey to come into view, and will not need to go far to achieve this.
- In rural areas, by contrast, a cat may have to wander several fields away to see any feline-related action.

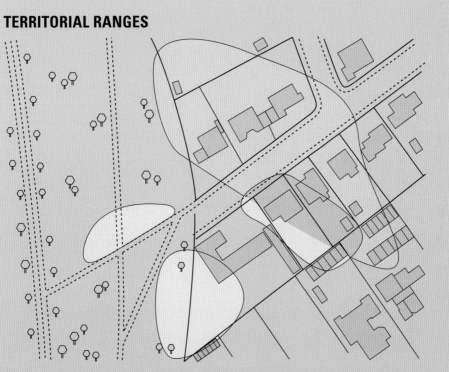

TERRITORIAL RANGES

The territorial ranges of two neutered cats, the male (shown in pale blue) and the female (shown in pale pink). These territorial ranges only overlap on the home ground.

Should my cat stay out all night?

Staying out all night is natural for nocturnal animals. They instinctively know that prey are around and that members of the opposite sex are also out and about. If a house cat remains out for more than 24 hours, then this could be cause for mild concern. If this behaviour is usual, then it is simply a part of a cat's personality. Hunting cats can obtain all the sustenance they require away from the home – and they might even enjoy the opportunities to interact with the rest of the local cat population.

Can my cat stay out in all weathers?

Cats have a fur coat to keep them warm and are equipped to survive normal weather conditions. Some breeds, such as the Norwegian Forest and Siberian Forest cats, are extremely hardy and can survive in rough conditions. A cat caught out in bad weather will want to return home as fast as possible. If it has explored too far to return home without being exposed to the worst of the weather, then it will instinctively seek out shelter under a car, shed or bush.

Is it all right to feed other cats that come into and around my home?

While it is certainly a kindness to offer other cats food, you may also be inadvertently increasing competition for your own cat. Encouraging others from the local cat population into the inner territory that belongs to a home cat can encourage it to develop aggressive or nervous behaviours.

My cat has been missing for several days. What is the best course of action?

Ideally, a search for a missing cat should begin in the twilight hours as this is when cats become more active and are more likely to be out and about. Your voice, calling the cat's name, will carry further into the night, and a cat that has become disorientated will recognize it and try to home in on the point of sound. It is worth repeating the calls at and beyond the edge of normal boundaries, because a cat that has been involved in a spat with another may flee the scene and become confused and disorientated.

There are also several other practical steps you can take:
- Ask cat-friendly neighbours if they have seen your cat during its period of absence – cats will happily sit on another doorstep if they feel a free meal and attention are the likely result. Ask your neighbours to keep an eye out for your cat.
- Put up notices in local shops, giving a clear description of your cat.
- Place an advertisement in the 'lost and found' section of your local newspaper.

Further details of how to entice a wandering cat home are given on page 69.

How can I encourage my wandering cat to return home?

There are a number of strategies to try.
- Enter your garden and name call (brightly) at regular intervals – every hour or more often. This is especially important in the early evening and beyond dusk. Do not be disheartened if your cat does not return immediately.
- You can expand this action to the outer borders of the known territory – streets, gardens, woods and so on.
- Clink a plate on the doorstep or ground outside at regular intervals – say, every two hours – and leave out a small morsel of strong-smelling food.
- Do not stand and watch unless from a discreet position as your cat will be able to see you and this may deter its return.

If you own a garden shed or bench, you can use this space to entice your cat home. Set a cat carrier or strong cardboard box on its side (keep the flaps) with a worn item of your old clothing inside so that your cat will recognize your scent. Place the box in the open shed, underneath it or under the bench. Observe the following guidelines:
- Do not use a carrier normally utilized for visits to the veterinary surgery as this may have a negative association for your cat.
- The cardboard box should not be too large – just big enough to support your curled-up cat, with the entrance hole just large enough to allow it to get in and out.
- The worn item will represent a scent link to you and act as a comfort blanket for your cat.

- It is important to ask your neighbours not to offer your cat shelter, interaction, food or play. Any offer of refuge away from your home may prove too attractive to counter.

Your cat's eventual return may depend on the weather, its personality and the availability of outside resources:
- If the weather is mild, warm and dry, a cat can survive for long periods away from home.
- If your cat has a feral background (this applies to many adopted cats) or has a strong hunter personality, then survival for long periods outdoors, even in poor and inhospitable weather, is possible, so bear this in mind and don't give up hope that it will never return.
- If your cat has found shelter and is a good hunter or is being fed by other people, these important resources for survival will extend its absence. Cats can remain outdoors for long periods – often several weeks – before eventually returning home.

Will my adopted cat try to go back to a previous home?

This depends entirely on the personality of the cat and the geography and distance between the old home and the new one. The territorial nature of cats means that they store mental maps of home territories and these can be used to return to a previous home. However, an adopted cat may have spent time in a boarding facility at a rehoming centre and will often have replaced the original memory map with another.

What can I do to stop my rescue cat wandering back to a previous home?

The simple answer is to provide a combination of food and comfort, and a happy home. A contented cat will not want to wander far from the place where creature comforts are never far away. If an adopted cat attempts to return to a previous area, it is important that the neighbours there do not offer it any food or shelter, as this support will discourage it from leaving the area. Try and talk to the neighbours to prevent this, if possible. It is wise to prevent the cat from obtaining access to outdoors during the first week or two after rehoming.

Should I insure my kitten?

Pet insurance has become a necessity for most cat owners. The sophistication of many policies now means that you can obtain a range of cover from basic veterinary costs to more unusual referrals to specialists. This becomes especially important if your kitten develops a physical or psychological problem later in life and your budget has not accounted for a veterinary surgeon's or behaviourist's charges. Not all policies cover the major aspects of potential treatment so make sure that you read the policy carefully so that you are aware of exactly what it covers. It is also important to compare like with like when it comes to policy costs. In general, the more you pay, the more aspects of pet treatment will be covered.

Should I have my kitten microchipped?

Yes, if a kitten is eventually to be allowed to roam freely outdoors. It is then essential that it not only wears a collar and a tag bearing your address, but is also microchipped. This up-to-date technology enables the relevant authorities or an examining veterinary surgeon to trace the owner when a cat becomes lost and is then recovered. Any method that speeds up the process of reuniting a pet with its owner is worth the investment.

The procedure involves using a special hand-held unit to implant a microchip in the neck of the cat. The tiny microchip has a unique identification code programmed into it, and this registration number is then added to a computer database that can be accessed by veterinary practices, relevant animal rescue groups and other authorities. In an emergency, should a cat become lost or injured, a hand-held scanner can be used to identify the owner code. This can then be used to give an enquirer the owner's name, address and contact telephone number.

Unlike a collar, which can become detached from the cat (particularly the quick-release collars that open if they become entangled), a microchip implant is always secure and will provide a permanent method of identification.

RIGHT **Microchipping a kitten means that its owner can be traced if it should get lost. It does not hurt or effect the kitten in any way.**

I need to rehome my cat. How can I find the best possible home for him?

The best home for your cat is yours. However, someone you know and trust may be the best person to adopt your cat if that becomes necessary. You could approach a close family member, a relative or a neighbour if the need to rehome is urgent. Failing that, you can contact rescue organizations and individuals who specialize in rehoming cats. However, these places are often full to the limit with cats and kittens that need a good home, so you may have to wait until they have space to accommodate your cat.

Can I take my cat with me to another country?

The laws on exporting cats depend on the destination country. Almost all countries have strict rules about the movement and importation of domestic animals. Your local veterinary practice will usually have access to the laws of the country in question, as they will usually have to examine and vaccinate the cat to conform to the legal requirements that are applicable in each case.

What happens at a cat show?

Cats shows are organized, usually annual events. Depending on the status of the show, professionals and cat owners can display their pets alongside others in order to compete to the physical standards of the various breeds and types, as interpreted by judges. Shows offer owners and breeders the opportunity to see other cats of the same and different breeds, and to compare their quality.

Championship shows for pedigree cats are taken seriously by the organizers, exhibitors and judges alike, whereas local, friendly pet shows usually have fewer rules and regulations to encourage ordinary owners with either pedigree or non-pedigree cats to exhibit.

Can I show my cat?

You will need to research show details and governing rules before entering any show, at whatever level. Otherwise, you could risk instant disqualification from the more professional events. Your local veterinary practice or cat fancy club will be able to offer relevant advice.

Would my cat be frightened by being at a cat show?

A cat that had never been to a show would certainly be confused and disorientated by the presence of so many other cats and people. In the case of a nervous individual, fear might take over. On the other hand, a contented cat might take to the show scene with no problem at all. Professional cat breeders and owners who are familiar with cat show routines introduce their cats to these events gradually or from an

early age. Once a cat learns that its life is not at risk at these events, it usually develops a calmer approach to the cat show procedures.

ABOVE Cat shows allow breeders and enthusiasts to compete against each other and promote their particular breed.

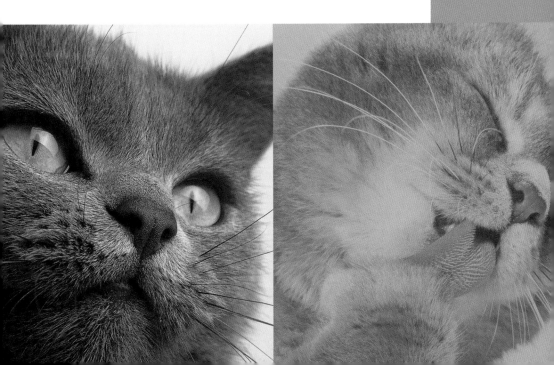

Physiology

Is it true that cats have flexible backbones?

Yes, a cat has a rather unique skeleton. Not only does it have more vertebrae in its backbone than a human, but this defining physiology also continues into the tail to create an extended backbone structure.

A cat's spine is made up of 30 vertebrae, excluding the 14–28 (depending on the breed) in the tail. These highly flexible vertebrae are divided between the neck (7), chest (13), back (7) and hip (3) and, alongside its strong muscular capabilities for jumping and propelling itself forward, help to make the cat dynamically sleek and fluid. As a result, cats are – in short bursts – one of the most balanced and fastest land predators on earth.

Is it true that cats can fall and not hurt themselves?

The answer to this depends largely on the height from which the cat falls and the surface on which it lands. The physics

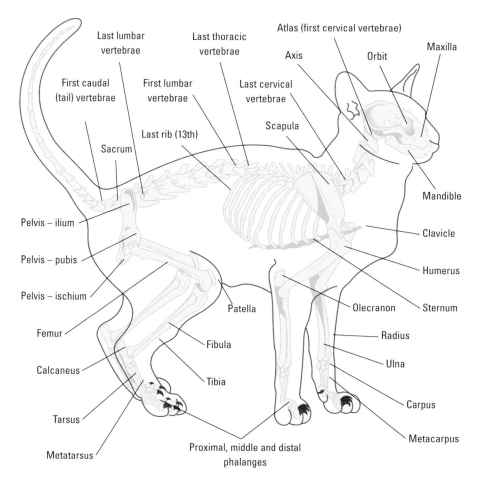

Last lumbar vertebrae

Last thoracic vertebrae

Atlas (first cervical vertebrae)

Axis

Orbit

Maxilla

First caudal (tail) vertebrae

First lumbar vertebrae

Last cervical vertebrae

Scapula

Last rib (13th)

Sacrum

Mandible

Pelvis – ilium

Clavicle

Pelvis – pubis

Humerus

Pelvis – ischium

Olecranon

Sternum

Patella

Femur

Radius

Fibula

Ulna

Calcaneus

Tibia

Tarsus

Carpus

Metatarsus

Proximal, middle and distal phalanges

Metacarpus

of dynamic muscle and bone structure, combined with quadruped capabilities and superior vision and inner-ear balance, means that a cat can quickly turn feet-first and then almost glide downwards, ready to land on all four feet. The plummeting cat realigns its head first, and then its spine and hindquarters, including the tail. This all takes place, instinctively, in a few split seconds.

If the descent is onto grass or leaf litter and soil – a fall from a tree, for example – the cat has a good chance of surviving a distance of about 15 m (50 ft) without much likelihood of physical injury. Cats can survive even greater falls, because the increased time in the descent allows for the gliding effect, wherein the cat relaxes, to come into play. Ironically, shorter falls can result in injury, because the cat will not have the descent time to allow for all the effects, from turning to gliding, to be brought into action.

When the cat lands, it is also protected from injury by its shock-absorbing feet and leg structure. A cat's paw pads consist of a tough epidermal (outer skin) layer connected to a compact area of sinewy tissue, and this combination acts to hold and connect the toe bones. The ankle bones are structured in such a way as to prevent lateral movement and are bound by ligaments for support. This ingenious physiological combination means that a cat can land safely, with its legs able to help absorb the full impact of a fall.

Why do cats have whiskers?

Facial whiskers, especially the antennae-like ones around the mouth, act as sensory extensions for cats. They are connected to receptors under the skin and are highly responsive to movement and possibly to olfactory stimulus as

OPPOSITE **The cat's skeleton.**

RIGHT **Facial whiskers enable cats to be sensitive to movement and temperature changes. They are used to help detect prey and to find their way around in the dark.**

well. It is widely believed that a cat can ascertain its ability to squeeze through extremely tight and reduced openings by whisker measurement. However, the bristly tufts of whisker hair around the face, plus the distinctive long mouth whiskers, are probably used more for sensory prey and competitor movement detection as they are incredibly sensitive to both movement and temperature changes. Measuring tight spaces is probably simply a secondary use for the elongated whiskers.

ABOVE **Receptors at the base of the facial whiskers provide a cat with important information about its surroundings.**

Can a cat 'talk' with its tail?

There is a basic language to be found in a cat's tail. A cat uses its tail primarily to aid balance during movement, but a secondary use is to communicate its intention to other cats:

- A tail that is lowered suggests that the cat is calm or submissive.
- A tail that is fully raised suggests that the cat is about to display a dominant form of behaviour such as marking or aggression.
- A tail that is repetitively swaying from side to side suggests that the cat is about to pounce in play or in attack against prey or competitor.

Can cats be 'left-paw biased', like left-handed people?

Research suggests that domesticated felines have a bias to a particular side. There is said to be a greater percentage of left-pawed cats than of left-handed humans. This may be connected to the fact that a cat has to be dextrous on all four legs. In order to do this, the cat has evolved to use both sides of the brain when maintaining balanced movement, mating or showing aggression. The quad-limb balance gives a cat the opportunity to have a preference, or it may be that one side of the brain is more stimulated than the other. This effect may give the cat the appearance of being left (front paw) biased. In any case, the cat, whether left or right pawed, is an accomplished climber, fast on land and a skilled hunter.

How do cats scent mark?

Cats are 'marking organisms' from head to tail (see below). However, the primary method of marking is to use urine and faeces, usually placed strategically to confirm perceived ownership of a territory. A height mark on a tree or an object is achieved with urine through a feline behaviour known as spraying. This behaviour is especially noticeable when entire toms and queens raise the tail and expel small bursts of urine. A fixed amount of urine is forced out and often enhanced with gland-scent to highlight territory ownership.

Spraying behaviour can also be displayed by neutered cats, although they tend to mark more with facial pheromones than with urine.

The largest wild cats, including lions and tigers as well as smaller species such as the lynx and the ocelot, can also be seen performing spraying behaviour in the wild.

ABOVE **A domesticated cat uses urine to mark its territory in exactly the same way as its wild cousins do in nature.**

Which part of its body does a cat use for scent marking?

Almost all parts of a cat's body are used to mark objects possessively, including owners. The head, flanks and the paws can be used, as well as the scent glands, most notably those in the anal area, to mark objects. In the wild, the objects for marking range from tufts of grass to tree trunks and offspring. It is possible that individual cats have their own scent 'fingerprint' that is recognized by competitors and kittens.

Is a cat's hearing better than ours?

A cat's hearing ability is actually on a par with a human's and at low frequencies, around 50 Hz, the thresholds are the same. However, cats are one of the most sensitive mammals to middle frequencies between 1 and 20 kHz. Cats are marginally more sensitive to higher frequencies than we are and can identify minute differences between slightly higher pitches. This sensitivity to higher-frequency sounds means that cats have slightly better hearing abilities than dogs.

A cat can hear sounds about two octaves higher than the highest note a human can perceive, and about half an octave higher than a dog. Both cats and dogs can detect a difference in pitch of between a fifth and a tenth of a tone. This ability is for prey detection and probably relates to the higher-pitched sounds of rodents and other ground-dwelling animals.

Is it true that white cats with blue or odd-coloured eyes are prone to deafness?

There is a recessive gene influence in white long- and short-haired cats that leads to inherited deafness – but not always. Experts commonly suggest that deafness in white cats is indicated by those with blue or odd-coloured eyes.

Is it true that white cats are more prone to skin cancer?

There are indications that pure white cats are more vulnerable to skin cancer caused by over-exposure to direct sunlight. Experts suggest that it is safer to keep a white cat in daytime shade during the brighter summer months. Sphynx cats (see page 48) and those with very short hair are more vulnerable to the adverse effects of sunlight.

BELOW All white cats are vulnerable to strong sunlight during the summer months. The ears and nose are particularly at risk of sunburn.

Is it true that cats don't see in colour?

Cats do not see exactly in 'full colour'. Although cats would appear to see the world almost in an overlapping binocular 'night vision' of greys, whites and blacks (when darkness falls, they need acute visual abilities), tests suggest that they can gradually discriminate between colours. Cats combine all their senses to 'feel' their way around, especially when hunting prey at night and, as with other predatory animals, may not need to be sensitive to colours to be successful predators.

Can cats see better than us?

We possess the same binocular vision as cats. However, our eyes are placed laterally parallel on our oblong-shaped face, giving us a slightly reduced fixed field of vision when compared to that of cats. The eyes of a cat are placed marginally to either side of its narrow face. Our overlapping vision covers roughly 210 degrees whereas a cat's is roughly 285 degrees.

Can cats see better than dogs?

Cats can see slightly better than dogs because their eye structure allows for some night vision. There is not a great deal of difference between feline and canine vision, although dogs generally have a narrower field of vision.

FIELDS OF VISION

A stereoscopic effect is created when the fields of vision of both eyes overlap.

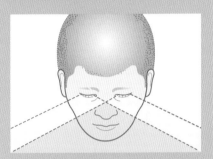

A human's fixed field of vision covers roughly 210 degrees, of which 120 is binocular overlap.

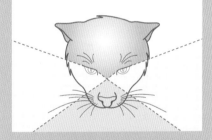

A cat's fixed field of vision covers roughly 285 degrees, of which 130 is binocular overlap.

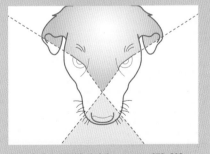

A dog's fixed field of vision covers 250–290 degrees, of which 80–110 is binocular overlap.

What makes cats' eyes reflect in the dark?

The eyes of a cat have a layer of reflective cells immediately behind the retina, known as the tapetum. Any light not absorbed by the microscopic rod-like structures in the back of the eye, especially when a cat's pupils are fully open, is passed back out. This process creates the distinctive, characteristic shine in the cat's eyes and is common to many land carnivores as well as seals.

Do cats yawn for the same reasons as humans?

Humans yawn as an uncontrolled or involuntary reaction to tiredness. The intake of air increases oxygen levels in the bloodstream and thence on to the brain. Cats yawn for the same reasons, but they also do this to stretch the muscles around the face and mouth. They may be triggered to do so by flehmening (see page 85).

Why do cats climb down trees backwards?

Although a cat may appear ungainly as it makes its way slowly down a tree trunk, tail first, this is the safest way for it to descend. The claws of a cat are curled forward to enhance its grip on trees when hunting or using elevation to seek refuge from other predators. The claws are not flexible in all directions, so by descending backwards it is easy for

ABOVE TOP A layer of reflective cells behind the retina make a cat's eyes shine in the dark.

ABOVE A cat yawns for the same reason as a human, but it is also a way to stretch their facial muscles.

RIGHT Climbing backwards is the safest way for a cat to come down a tree.

the cat to maintain a secure hold and reach the ground safely.

Why is a cat's tongue so rough to the touch?

The abrasive surface of a cat's tongue is covered with many tiny, hooked 'papillae' – almost like miniature teeth. These hooks have a dual purpose, enabling the cat to clean off any flesh from the bones of prey as well as enhancing grooming.

Why do cats sometimes grimace or grin?

The grinning cat, or one that is flexing its nose and lip, is performing a physical reaction known as 'flehmening'. Flehmen behaviour is believed to be a direct response to pheromones and other natural body-chemical odours, and is triggered when there is stimulation in an area behind the nasal area known as the vomero-nasal or Jacobson's organ. This facial behaviour occurs more frequently in the big cats, which tend to possess a more developed vomero-nasal organ.

Are male tortoiseshell cats sterile?

Tortoiseshell cats of any breed are known to lack the X chromosome. The colour is therefore an indication that the cat has a condition that would normally lead to its being sterile. However, some tortoiseshell males will not be pure and may possibly be fertile. Professional breeders, line breeding with male and female cats carrying the desired, distinctive markings, will work for years with generations of cats in order to obtain the lovely tortoiseshell kittens that are as expensive as they are delightful. (See also page 22.)

What is awn hair?

Awn hair is a distinctive form of bristly hair that lies within the undercoat of a cat. It is often described as short tufted fur with thickened tips. Its function is to protect the skin from cold and damp, and the cat can quickly groom it dry with its tongue.

Do all cats moult?

To a greater or lesser extent, all cats lose hair, especially in the summer months when they need less insulation from the weather. Logic dictates that long-haired cats moult more hairs than their short-haired counterparts, but this is not always the case. Some more active outdoor cats shed more hairs indoors than more sedentary house cats.

RIGHT Developing a fertile male Tortoiseshell normally requires years of selective breeding. Most Tortoiseshells are female.

5

Caring for
Your Cat

What is the optimum age at which a kitten should leave its litter mother and siblings?

Opinions vary on this. Most feline behaviourists agree that the ideal age for a kitten to be passed to a prospective owner is between 7 and 9 weeks. Many professional pedigree cat breeders release kittens at 12 weeks, arguing that the kittens are much more socialized to each other and have been introduced to and handled frequently by humans. Many rescue kittens have been influenced negatively by early separation from the litter mother (prior to or at 6 weeks), as well as by the potential of feral influence in the original mating that produced the litter. This is either because owners bring a litter of unwanted kittens into the rescue centre too early or, when they are first discovered, the kittens are often assumed to have been abandoned when the litter mother is actually away or is trying to lure investigators away from the nest area.

The kittens' learning process will continue for as long as the litter mother remains with them. Extended time with the litter mother and siblings often improves socialization with and tolerance towards other cats, which can be important in later life. Basic skills developed by extended interaction with the litter mother include stalking, pouncing and prey-kill behaviour, which

KITTEN DEVELOPMENT

Age	Behaviour
0–2 weeks	Kittens are blind and deaf. The litter mother suckles them, licks them frequently and is very protective.
3 weeks	Litter mother and kittens begin to interact. She grooms them, and prevents them from becoming over-demanding and aggressive. Kittens begin to explore just outside the kittening box.
4 weeks	Kittens begin accepting semi-solid foods and can be taught to use a litter tray placed close to the kittening box.
6 weeks	Kittens are learning through play. They explore progressively further away from the kittening box.
8 weeks	Kittens are fully weaned onto solid food. First vaccinations can be given around this time.

are taught through feline play activity. Kittens should be introduced to as many aspects of human life as possible to help in future socialization with their new owners.

Will a new kitten miss its litter mother and siblings?

Initially, the answer must be yes. The first few days are probably confusing and disorientating for the kitten, without its litter mother and fellow kittens to offer reassurance and familiarity. This is despite the fact that the litter mother naturally spends less and less time with her kittens as they grow older (and because they are weaned onto solid foods,

they spend less time with her). She has to build up her strength again after sacrificing much energy and effort in bringing up her offspring. The mating tom has no further interest in her, and none at all in his descendants.

The kittens barely miss each other as they gradually leave, because fewer litter members mean more food and attention for those that remain.

However, your healthy, developing kitten is young and adaptable, and is ready to find its place in the world. Its new territory (home and surroundings) is full of exciting new discoveries and adventures. There are some threats and fears, but a contented and healthy kitten will find that its curiosity has few boundaries. The owner, as 'replacement litter mother' or 'lead cat', will help to introduce the world to a kitten as safely and confidently as possible.

What accessories are required for the first journey home?

The first essential is a cat carrier (see page 90). You will also need a clean towel and kitchen roll or newspaper on the bottom of the carrier to soak up any mishaps that may occur. It is a good idea to take a family member or a friend with you, whose job it is to concentrate on the needs of the kitten while you drive (or to drive while you look after the kitten).

LEFT Young kittens soon learn to be independent when removed from their mother. Kittens usually go to their new homes when they are 7–9 weeks old.

ABOVE **A metal carrier offers a simple, safe option when transporting cats. The more used they are to a carrier, the less disturbing they will find it.**

How should I transport a new kitten to my home?

Cats and kittens should be transported in a special cat carrier. There are both economy and luxury versions available. A warm towel placed inside the carrier will create a safe haven for the kitten, which will have no real concept about the journey or its new home. It is important to use a cat carrier because a frightened kitten may panic when first placed in a vehicle with someone unfamiliar.

Pick up the kitten gently by supporting its bottom with one hand, and place it in the carrier, close the door quickly and secure the fastener. Position the carrier on your or your helper's knees to prevent any sudden movements causing the carrier and kitten to be thrown about. It is important not to leave the kitten unattended while it is inside the carrier. It is also vital to make sure that it cannot become either too hot or too cold.

This will usually be the first time the kitten has travelled in a car, and the experience will probably be extremely frightening for a young cat. It will also be the first time it has been separated from its litter siblings and this separation, too, can induce fearfulness.

What basic equipment do I need for my new kitten?

There are just a few essential items you will need to assemble before you bring your new kitten home.
- Food bowl
- Water bowl
- Litter tray
- Collar
- Cat bed

For grooming (especially for long-haired cats):
- Fine- and wide-toothed combs
- Soft and hard brushes
- Hand glove brush
- Soft cloth or chamois

Optional:
- Claw clippers
- Bowl or baby bath (see page 106).

ABOVE **Supervise the introduction of young children to kittens and cats to ensure their relationship starts on a calm basis.**

Where should I introduce my kitten to its new home?

Once home, place the cat carrier and kitten in the room that has been chosen for the first night. A small room is less daunting to a disorientated kitten, although the unfamiliarity of the layout, structures and scents will test the fearlessness of any feline, young or old. At this stage it is important to close any doors and windows that, if left open, might offer a frightened kitten the opportunity to take flight. If you don't ensure that the early location and surroundings are secure, you may find yourself searching for a kitten that has disappeared into the undergrowth, shed or under a car – a somewhat daunting task, especially at night.

How can I help my new kitten to settle into my home?

The most important thing you can do is to avoid exposing your kitten to everyone and everything at once. It is not necessary to make introductions on the first day. Ideally, in the initial 24 hours the kitten should be allowed to rest and explore in one room, which should be made secure from other animals and be visited by only a minimal number of people.

When and how should my children be introduced to the kitten?

Infants and small children should always be supervised during encounters with a new kitten. This will prevent the possibility of any rough handling and accidental aggression or undue attention by either party.

Once you are confident that the kitten has begun to settle, you can then encourage individual family members to enter the room one at a time and wait until the newcomer approaches them. This 'controlled' method of introducing the kitten to new people will make this potentially scary situation gentle and less stressful for the kitten. After a couple of days, or when the kitten appears more sociable, subsequent introductions can be less formal.

ABOVE Most adult cats will find the introduction of a kitten to their home non-threatening. Keep a close eye on their first few meetings.

How should I introduce a kitten to our existing cat?

This depends very much on the nature of the adult cat that is already a member of your family. If it is confident, contented and non-aggressive, there is little danger of it finding a defenceless kitten too threatening, although that can all change as the kitten develops to maturity. It is advisable to allow a meeting of the two with some casual and calm supervision. If everything goes smoothly, the kitten may even curl up to the cat (replacement litter mother), or an adult female cat may become maternal towards the kitten (replacement offspring).

On the other hand, a nervous or insecure adult cat will initially want to see off the new intruder that is regarded as a potential competitor for food, territory and access to a loving owner. Such a nervous adult cat would need to be put in a cat carrier or crate and, with the use of a harness, exposed to the kitten very slowly and carefully over a period of time.

How should I introduce a kitten to our other pets?

The most likely pet a kitten will have to get to know is a dog. If you know that yours is friendly towards cats, play a brief retrieval game with the dog on a lead in the same room while the kitten is exploring. However, if your dog shows aggression or hyperactivity towards cats, then muzzle it as a precaution. A dog that displays positive behaviour towards a kitten should be rewarded with special food treats.

It is not ideal to keep a dog and a kitten (or cat) permanently separated in the home. There will always come a time when they are accidentally brought together, with possibly disastrous consequences. For this reason, it is important that 'controlled socialization', with food rewards to both parties for good behaviour, is undertaken over the settling-in period.

If you have small pets such as indoor rabbits and guinea pigs, then brief and controlled interactive introductions can be made after the kitten has been resident for a week or two.

Should I offer food and water to help my kitten settle down?

Several things should be available to the kitten right from the start.
- Water.
- Small amount of food.
- Litter tray (a covered tray, in the case of an adult cat).
- Most important of all: plenty of peace and quiet.

If the cat is adopted, it is a good idea to ask the rescue centre or previous owner for a small amount of soiled litter material. Transferring this waste to the new litter tray will ensure that the cat has an immediate association with its new surroundings through scent, and often encourages it to use the tray.

Should I stroke my kitten a lot in the first days to help it bond with me?

There is always a great temptation to pick up a new kitten continually and stroke it until the fur almost comes out. However, although it is important to have positive physical contact with a kitten, this contact should be undertaken

confidently and correctly (see below) if the relationship is to develop without promoting dependency.

While a small kitten is fairly easy to scoop up, it is important that you support it fully, with one hand holding its hindquarters and the other gently holding its body. A cuddle session while seated in a chair will often encourage the kitten to take a much-needed cat nap.

When my kitten cries, should I go and pick it up?

Instinct encourages us to go to a kitten when it cries. This is because maternal and paternal behaviour is part of the

ABOVE It is possible to learn how to distinguish a cat's different cries and establish whether they are from hunger, fear or attention-seeking.

human social behaviour that would be directed towards an infant. A young kitten can easily learn to manipulate a concerned response from its owner and could then cry at every desire, from being hungry to wanting attention. In this way, over-dependency on the kitten's part is quickly encouraged.

It is possible to identify different types of kitten cries in the same way as with a human baby. A mother instinctively learns which cry relates to:

- Genuine hunger (by linking it with feeding patterns).
- Attention-seeking (just been fed and made comfortable).
- Genuine distress (higher-pitched cry).

You can learn to distinguish between the different cries of a kitten and will then know which can be ignored (the cries will then stop) and which require an appropriate response (owner attention).

Is it all right to allow my kitten to explore my home freely?

A confident kitten is far more likely to explore and taste new substances than an adult cat. Older animals will have learned what is safe and what should be avoided, while youngsters are often more active and inquisitive. A kitten will encounter more new aspects in a home than an adult cat.

The kitchen is probably the most dangerous area for any cat. This room also has an attractive association, because it is where food is prepared and made available. Unfortunately, the kitchen also includes hot surfaces and pans filled with boiling water, and is home to sharp

BELOW Some kittens are adventurous and allow their curiosity to lead them into dangerous places.

knives, plastic bags, rubbish bins (containing a frightening array of dangerous items such as sharp tins and glass), household detergents and the washing machine. Any of these items can become a trap for an exploring kitten.

To prevent a kitten accessing the kitchen, it may be wise to install a child gate, completely covered with a mesh barrier. Although an adult cat could probably use various platforms to launch itself over most heights, it is unlikely that a kitten would attempt to climb great heights and make such a leap to overcome the gate.

It is highly unlikely that an adult cat would attempt to eat a poisonous or toxic houseplant. A kitten, however, may be tempted to lick or nibble on a leaf, so exclude or remove such plants (see page 102). Any detergents or medicines should be kept in closed cupboards to avoid possible accidents.

When should I allow my kitten to go outside for the first time?

First of all, your kitten must be given all the necessary vaccinations. After this, you can allow supervised excursions into the immediate garden or yard territory. Make the initial explorations brief and interactive, with food treats and clicker training (see page 166), so that a positive association is made with the outside world. In any case, an adventurous kitten will probably already have been crying to make a visit outdoors, especially if it has caught a tantalizing glimpse of other cats through the patio doors.

ABOVE **Before you allow your cat loose to explore the great outdoors for the first time, it is important to make sure that it has had all the necessary vaccinations and inoculations.**

Do I need to register my kitten at a veterinary practice?

There is no law that states an owner has to register a pet with a veterinary surgeon. However, you will need to visit a veterinary practice for your kitten's protective vaccination programme. And, it can be extremely useful and save time in an emergency if a veterinary practice holds your details and also those of your kitten.

How should I transport my kitten to the veterinary surgery?

It is always advisable to use a cat carrier to transport a kitten (or cat) to the surgery. This is for safety reasons, both in

ABOVE It is important to have a new kitten examined by a veterinary surgeon.

the vehicle and in the waiting room of the practice. There can be a rich assortment of pets in the surgery and some dogs can be extremely boisterous, others even aggressive towards cats.

Can I change to another veterinary practice?

It is entirely your decision to register your pet with a particular veterinary practice. Your cat's medical records can easily be transferred from one practice to another, provided that you offer the details of your previous veterinary practice to the next.

Do I need permission from my veterinary surgeon to change to another practice?

No, permission is not necessary, although your existing practice may appreciate knowing the reason for the change. This can be because of a house move, costs, an individual's preferences or for a second opinion. In the latter case, while few professionals enjoy having their decisions questioned, it is not unreasonable for owners to want the best care and attention for their pets.

ABOVE **A kitten will shed most of its hairs while sleeping. It makes sense if it has its own bed as this makes it easy to dispose of the hairs.**

Does my kitten need a bed?

A kitten would have little difficulty finding a cosy place to sleep, even if you have not provided a purpose-made bed. Favourites include in the airing cupboard, on a human bed or sofa, and under radiators.

Nevertheless, it is a good idea to provide a kitten with a bed, because it is there, during both sleeping and waking hours, that most hairs will be shed. It is undoubtedly preferable for hairs to be cast in the cat bed than in one of the family beds.

What type of cat bed is best?

There is a wide variety of beds available for a cat to sleep in. The range includes wicker baskets, igloos made from fabric (similar to a tent), bean bags, and even hammocks that can be hung on heated radiators. A cat bed should be warm, snug and easy to clean, and is best positioned in a quiet, draught-free place in the home.

How much food does a indoor kitten need?

The type and quantity of food varies greatly with the age of the kitten. From 4 to 6 weeks a kitten should be eating moist food, after which it can be given a combination of mostly solid foods (fresh, tinned or dried), although one feed can still consist of a paste based on special cat milk and baby kitten food. By the time a kitten is 8 weeks old it should be fully weaned onto solid foods. The following months should see a gradual reduction in the number of feeds to two or three larger meals per day. An indoor kitten's feed requirements are summarized in the table on page 98.

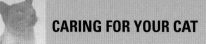

INDOOR KITTEN FEEDING GUIDE

Age	Food	Frequency
0–3 weeks*	Consult a vet, breeder or rescue centre expert. The kitten will require a substitute for its mother's milk plus a vitamin and mineral supplement.	Consult an expert.
4–6 weeks	1 teaspoon or slightly more of liquid-consistency kitten food mixed with baby milk substitute.	4–5 times a day.
6–12 weeks	2–3 large teaspoons of solid kitten food (tinned moist and semi-moist, or dried).	4–5 times a day.
3–6 months	Increased quantities of solid foods.	Scaling down from 5 to 2–3 times a day.

*Kittens should not be removed from the litter at this age, because interruption of normal socialization can lead to nutritional deficiencies and behavioural problems in the adult cat.

How much food does an outdoor kitten need?

An active kitten will burn up more calories than an indoor kitten. It will need extra protein to help with body and muscle growth spurts encouraged by the high levels of exercise. Gradually increase the food quantities suggested in the table for an indoor kitten (see left), until it is obvious from the excess food remaining that the kitten is receiving sufficient.

Is a scratching post really necessary?

It is natural for a cat to scratch an upright object such as a tree in nature, in order to scent mark its territory. Because of this, if you do not have an appropriate target for this behaviour you will be asking for the cat to be destructive towards walls, doors, door frames, furniture and furnishings. (See also pages 164–165.)

ABOVE **Cats scent-mark when they scratch a vertical post. This behaviour can counter inappropriate damage and other marking in the home.**

What is a litter tray?

A litter tray is effectively an indoor toilet for your cat. It acts as a replacement for the place where the cat would usually perform these functions outdoors. An outdoor cat would toilet in loose soil or leaf litter and, unless deliberately middening (where faeces are exposed for territorial purposes – see page 171), would cover up its wastes. For practical, health and feline privacy reasons, covered litter trays are best.

What type of litter material is best?

Although there are many litter materials available, the best is the one a cat willingly uses. Materials range from economic wood and paper chips to expensive dolomite varieties – based on usage, the best may be the fine, granular 'clumping litter'. This material is also easy to clean, as the results of a cat's toileting are absorbed, clumped and easily isolated from the whole tray.

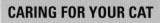

ABOVE It is important to replace soiled litter material for cat health. Change the litter frequently and wash the container with a mild solution of bleach.

LEFT Housebound cats need to have access to a litter tray at all times. You will find a selection of trays and types of litter in all good pet shops.

Do I really need to offer my kitten an indoor litter tray?

A kitten that is house-bound in the early stages will need an indoor litter tray. However, a healthy adult cat that is an active outdoor type will not normally require an 'indoor toilet', as most (if not all) its toileting will be performed outside.

How can I encourage my new kitten to use its litter tray?

It is a good idea to place a kitten that is just waking up directly into the tray. Instinct will often take over as it moves its paws around the litter material. Once a kitten has used a tray once, it will instinctively try to 'over-mark' its own toilet scents. If a kitten has soiled on newspaper, small amounts of this can be transferred to the tray to create the first 'marking' process on its behalf.

How often do I need to change the soiled litter material?

It is wise to change litter material that has been exposed to an adult cat on a daily basis. Young kittens will not usually produce copious amounts of urine and faeces, and it can be useful not to over-clean the tray in the early days to encourage its use.

Cats are very clean animals. To maintain an adult cat in good health it is important to ensure that its litter tray is always kept clean.

Does my new kitten need a collar?

A collar is the most economical way to attach an identification disc, tag or fob to a kitten. The better types are made from leather or from man-made, durable synthetic material. They should be fitted lightly rather than tightly onto the neck. A contact telephone number or abbreviated address can be engraved onto a disc or placed inside a barrel holder, which is attached to the collar.

There are many types of collar available:

- Quick-release or safety designs that have an elasticated section are the safest products and are worth the extra investment.
- A young kitten that is restricted to the home could be fitted with a soft fabric collar (not a flea collar), to help it to become comfortable wearing one. Once established as everyday wear, collars can be upgraded in size as the cat grows. Check the collar every day to make sure that it isn't too small.
- A soft flea collar is designed for semi-adult to adult cats and is not suitable for kittens. There is more danger of a soft collar on an adventurous kitten becoming hooked onto a point, creating a restriction that could easily lead to strangulation.

ABOVE **Toys represent replacement-prey and can be used for positive owner-interaction. Cats love playing with small lightweight balls and other little toys.**

Does my kitten need toys?

Kittens need interaction rather than a box of toys. Simple devices, such as toy fishing rods with a catnip-sprayed (see page 178) toy mouse on one end, could offer a kitten frequent fun, with the owner reeling it in and casting it out. Kittens will play with any object that catches their fancy and a table tennis ball should never be underestimated. A kitten will instinctively treat some objects as pretend prey and will pounce on, throw, catch, turn upside down, pat and bite even a piece of discarded screwed-up newspaper.

What are the best type of cat toys to buy?

The best cat toys are those that require little interaction with an owner. These will be useful for keeping the cat busy during periods when it is alone in the

home. Track toys and mechanical devices that send toy mice flying in circles are excellent (see page 176–177), although they are more expensive than the simple toys that you can play with together.

ABOVE Some new toys do not require interaction from owners so are ideal for cats alone in the day.

Are some houseplants poisonous to my cat?

Some houseplants are thought to be potentially poisonous to a kitten. Ivy (*Hedera*), Christmas cherry (*Solanum capsicastrum*), poinsettia and philodendron are some popular plants that it is probably best to avoid.

Are some garden plants poisonous to my cat?

Some trees, such as laburnum, produce poisonous seeds, so ideally these should be removed or access to them restricted. Some shrubs and other plants are also thought to be poisonous to cats, including:
• Azaleas
• Sweet peas (*Lathyrus odoratus*)
• Oleander
• Lupins

- Delphiniums
- Rhododendrons
- Clematis
- Fuchsia

Although a cat is unlikely to eat such plants, it is best if a cat-friendly garden is not heavily stocked with them.

What grooming accessories do I need?

It is wise to invest in good quality brushes and combs, because they will be in regular use – especially if your cat is a long-haired breed. There are glove-type brushes, soft and hard brushes, and a range of fine- to broad-toothed combs. The best are easy on the hand and comfortable to use, so take time to handle the accessories before making a purchase.

Do I need to groom my cat every day?

This depends on whether the cat is long- or short-haired. Generally, a short-haired cat rarely needs to be brushed on a daily basis unless it will be attending a show. An average indoor house cat should be brushed at least once a week. An adventurous outdoor cat, which is more likely to come into contact with natural debris, would probably benefit from being groomed twice a week. For long-haired cats, see page 104.

BELOW Some plants such as fuchsia are potentially dangerous to cats, as are some trees, shrubs and garden plants.

BELOW Regular grooming is essential for the well-cared for cat, especially if it has long hair. There is a good selection of brushes and combs to choose from.

How often should I groom my long-haired cat?

This depends on whether the cat is an indoor type or an active, outdoor one. However, to prevent the build-up of fur balls (that are a consequence of self-grooming), knots and tangles, and to reduce the amount of hair shed at any one time, it is advisable to brush a long-haired cat every day.

Do my cat's claws need clipping on a regular basis?

This will depend on how active the cat is and whether you live in a rural or urban area. An outdoor cat in an urban setting that is continually on the prowl will

ABOVE Regular daily grooming can help to prevent fur balls and a tangled coat – especially important for long-haired cats.

naturally wear down its claws. This cat will also be using its claws to mark fences, and street and garden trees. The rural counterpart of this cat will do less road work but some scratching in woodland regions.

By comparison, an indoor cat will not have the same opportunities as its more active outdoor cousins and will need its growing claws clipped, both for owner handling safety and to restrict the amount of potential damage achieved by indoor marking.

Check the length of your cat's claws every few months. Provided the claws are not cut back to the quick and appropriate clippers are used, the procedure should become fairly straightforward as the cat gets used to it, especially if started from an early age. Clipping cat claws should be undertaken confidently, yet still erring on the side of caution. Have a styptic pencil to hand in case of bleeding. Otherwise it is a procedure that is best left to your veterinary surgeon.

Should I bath my cat?

This depends mainly on whether the cat is an indoor sedate type or an active, outdoor one. Active cats come into contact with far more dirt than indoor cats, which remain cleaner for longer. Cats' grooming behaviour goes back to their wild ancestors which needed to be in excellent condition to hunt and compete with the rest.

It is easier to wipe down a dusty cat with a large, soft cotton cloth dipped in lukewarm water than it is to give it a bath. However, if a cat has got itself particularly dirty, bathing may be necessary. Although most cat breeds are notoriously phobic about water – the Turkish Van being one exception (see page 32) – it is possible to wash a cat if this procedure has been done from an early age so that the animal knows what is happening and will tolerate it, even though it will still not like the procedure.

ABOVE Indoor cats require regular claw trimming, particularly of the front claws. Use claw clippers with a spring handle.

LEFT Cats, especially those who go outdoors, need to be groomed everyday to keep them free from fur knots, dirt and potential pollutants.

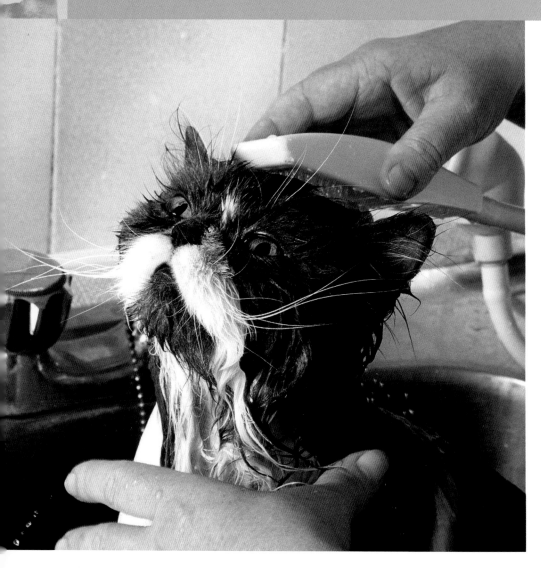

How should I bath my cat?

The easiest method is to use a shower-rose. There are a number of guidelines to observe:
- Make absolutely sure that the water temperature does not exceed lukewarm at any time.
- Soak the cat from behind, holding its underside gently but firmly.
- Use a non-toxic, mild baby shampoo or

ABOVE The careful use of a handheld showerhead can often be the easiest way to bathe a cat. Use lukewarm water and a mild shampoo.

a pet shampoo, although it is always best to avoid using any soap product around a cat's head and eyes. Do not use excessive amounts of shampoo – you could pre-mix a solution of mild shampoo and water into a measuring jug to prevent any excess from coming into contact with the cat.

- Avoid being too vigorous with the 'scrubbing'.
- Make sure you rinse off all shampoo with lukewarm water.
- Gently dry the cat with a towel in a warm house, then allow the cat to finish off drying itself while restricted to the bathroom so that it doesn't shake water everywhere. If the home is not warm, carefully blow-dry the fur with a hair dryer on a cool setting. If the cat becomes amenable to this drying procedure it will be possible to brush groom the coat dry – gentle brushing opens up the coat to the air and this promotes drying.
- It is a good idea to keep a baby bath especially for the purpose of bathing your cat or kitten, because it is easier to hold a kitten in a small container within the bath or on stool.

Bathing can help to rid a cat of most loose hairs and will make grooming with combs and brushes much easier. Some cat owners, especially those who show their pets, bath and shampoo them on a regular basis.

Can I use human soaps and shampoos on my cat?

Most human soap products should not be used on animals. This is because they contain scents and other ingredients that can trigger serious dermatological conditions. Cats maintain a healthy balance between skin and hair with natural oils, and aggressive cleaning

compounds can have an adverse effect by removing these.

Products developed for sensitive human skin types, including many baby soaps, could be used carefully and would not harm a cat. However, if you want to be completely confident it is advisable to use products developed specifically for cats which are available from pet stores.

Are there other methods for cleaning my cat's coat?

It is possible to clean a short- to medium-haired cat's coat using bran. In effect, you are giving the cat a dry bath by rubbing warm bran into its coat. This must be followed by a brushing and combing session to ensure that all of the bran is removed.

What should I do to treat my cat's dandruff?

Some cats produce what appears to be dry and flaky skin that looks like dandruff. This condition is caused by the microscopic mite *Cheyletiella* and should be treated with a special medical or pet shampoo that is known to kill parasites. After a light wash, rinse off thoroughly in lukewarm water and then brush and comb the cat's coat.

There are other dermatological conditions that may also encourage fur loss and skin inflammation, so if any of these symptoms are observed you should take your cat to be examined by a veterinary surgeon.

RIGHT Cats and household chemicals should be kept well apart. Store cleaning items in a cupboard that your cat can't open.

LEFT The correct way to hold a kitten is by carefully supporting the whole of its body with both your hands.

What is the best way to handle my cat?

Although we all like to pick up and handle cats, it is not a necessary part of the relationship. As if to prove the point, some strong-minded cats will react adversely to be handled. Fortunately for most cat owners, a contented cat will not consider its dignity has been unduly compromised if it is handled correctly.

A cat should be picked up in a two-handed movement, with one hand supporting the hindquarters and the other supporting the forward part of the body between the front legs. This allows for a chin tickle at the same time.

Is it possible to lead-walk a cat outdoors?

It is certainly possible to teach a cat or kitten to walk on a lead. Some personalities and breeds will be easier to lead-walk than others.

Lead-training a cat is a gradual process. First, the cat will need to become accustomed to wearing a harness as initially it will be unused to the restraint. Place the harness on the cat for short periods while it is in the house. Then, when it is comfortable with the harness, attach the lead for short periods and lead the cat around the house. It is important not to try immediately to 'walk' the cat outdoors at this stage. After a while, try walking the cat around the garden. Then go for a walk in the great outdoors. Time and patience will lead to success.

Will leaving upstairs windows open encourage my cat to fall out of them?

A large, wide-open window might encourage a young cat to make mistakes. An adult cat, however, would never 'leap' out of an open window unless it was being pursued. An upper-frame window, usually much smaller than the main window, can be left open for room ventilation. Only a cat that knows its capabilities and has learned to enter and exit via windows would leap up to a small open window to exit a home.

How do I make my house safe for my cat?

Making a home safe for a cat is similar to taking precautions for a young child. There are a number of issues to address: **Detergents and other household chemicals** Although a cat is unlikely to lick up a solution, it could easily knock over a bottle and then walk through the spilt liquid. Once a chemical finds its way onto the cat's paws it could begin to irritate its sensitive skin or, worse, be digested when the cat attempts to clean itself. Keep all chemicals safely stored away in cupboards.

Electric cables Any exposed cables are a potential hazard for a playful kitten. Make sure they are not frayed, because if a kitten begins to play with an unsafe lead it can easily be electrocuted.

Windows A cat can be given safe access to the house through a ground-floor window. Apart from this, make sure that all windows are secure (see page 109). There is always the possibility that a kitten could escape through an open window on an upper floor and be seriously injured in a fall.

Sharp implements Household items such as knives, drawing pins and needles should be kept safely out of reach of a kitten or cat inside drawers or hung on hooks on the wall.

Fireplaces These provide access to chimneys and can become traps for an inquisitive kitten. Be sure to block them off for the first 6–12 months.

How do I make my garden safe for my cat?

Few gardens are unsafe for cats. This is because they know to avoid water and general debris by exploring cautiously and walking gingerly on uneven surfaces. However, there are some specific hazards to avoid:

Industrial-type debris Materials from building work or car repair, open drain covers and inspection pits offer obvious dangers to cats.

Poisonous plants It is wise to avoid planting flora that are known to be poisonous to cats (see page 102). although these are unlikely to be a real barrier to a cat that enjoys roaming in the garden.

Tools and toxic materials Garden chemicals, such as pesticides, and sharp gardening equipment should always be locked away safely.

Garden ponds These are potential disaster areas for young cats. A pond should not have steep sides that would be difficult for a cat to climb if it accidentally fell into the water. You could place a net over the water or construct a low fence around the pond to prevent your young cat from gaining access. Netting has the secondary benefit of reducing the number of leaves entering and polluting the water.

What is a cat run?

A cat run is an outdoor, free-standing structure or pen, at first sight resembling an aviary. It provides a safe environment in which a cat or cats can enjoy the opportunity to explore and bask in the sunshine and fresh air, and provides peace of mind for you.

Cat runs are usually made up of netting panels on all sides, including the roof. Most cat runs are of a modest size and are either free-standing or attached directly to the rear of the house. The latter arrangement enables house cats to enter directly from an open window, door or cat flap. Larger cat runs are designed to house a number of cats and can cover the whole garden or yard space, creating a safe, enclosed territory for companion cats to enjoy.

Is it cruel to keep a cat away from the great outdoors in a run, or shut in the home?

All cats naturally want and enjoy the freedom to wander outdoors and climb trees, to scent and to interact with other cats. Cats especially enjoy lazing in a warm, sunny spot in the garden – and anyone who has watched a kitten chasing flies from flower to flower will know that a garden is home to a cat. Preventing a cat from playing and resting in the garden may seem strange to those who do not worry about where their cats stray. Indeed, many people consider keeping a cat permanently indoors to be rather cruel and, at the very least, imagine the owner guilty of promoting an unnatural situation.

To anyone unfamiliar with the ways of house cats, it may well appear harsh to restrict them to the home or a run. However, cat personalities differ widely and some contented cats will thrive in the reduced territory of the home, sometimes with the addition of an outdoor run. An adventurous or hunter cat would undoubtedly prefer to explore the surrounding area, and such a cat would find being enclosed in a restrictive space extremely frustrating.

Nevertheless, kittens that are brought up from an early age to live exclusively in the house and a run are usually content with a reduced territory. They soon adapt to home life and often feel secure in the knowledge that they are protected from the outside world. One drawback of housebound cats is that they can become extremely attached to their owners and may develop over-dependency – although some owners do enjoy such an intense level of bonding and neediness from their cats.

What are the benefits of a cat run?

There are a number of advantages to a cat run. A run offers owners security and protection for:
- Vulnerable cats.
- Expensive pedigree cats.
- Cats in a high urban feline population.
- Cats in areas with a high density of road traffic.
- Cats in areas with a feral cat population and therefore an increased risk of infection.

When a kitten has become dearly loved by a family, often the idea of giving it complete freedom to roam has worrying implications. Feral cats often carry diseases such as cat 'flu, as well as fleas and worms, and they can wander in and out of any garden. Some toms and feral cats can also be extremely territorial and aggressive towards house cats. The highly tuned instincts of these cats can make house cats territorially insecure if they are continually confronted. Exposure to aggressive cats increases the likelihood of indoor 'marking' behaviours such as spraying and inappropriate defecating in the home.

With the huge increase of traffic in recent years, the biggest threat to a cat probably comes from road accidents. It may only be a climb and a drop away from your garden to a major road. Sadly,

because of the flexibility of a cat's physique, many road traffic accidents result in feline fatalities. It is very difficult (if not impossible) to protect an outdoor cat from the heavy traffic that regularly uses our roads today.

A cat run ensures that cats are guarded against road traffic, as well as aggression and competition from other outside cats.

How large should a cat run be?

Plan your cat run as large as possible. A run cannot be too large for young, healthy cats – some owners even enclose their entire garden! When budgeting the cost of an enclosure, remember that the cat run will require a roof section. A door panel should also be included, in order to provide easy access to the run for cleaning and maintenance.

There are few hard-and-fast rules about the actual size of a cat run, because most cats will make full use of any space

ABOVE A properly constructed cat run can provide a safe outdoor haven, especially for valuable pedigree cats and other town-based pets.

offered. A single cat would thrive in a run the size of a modest garden shed. However, an elongated shape would offer both design opportunities in the layout and more variety of movement for an active cat.

Where is the best place to install a cat run?

One of the most important factors to consider in siting a run is how the cat will access it. If the run is to be attached directly to a door in the house wall, then the run should be placed there and a cat flap installed to allow the cat to wander freely between the house and the run.

If it is not practical to install a cat flap, then it is possible to give access to the run via a window. In this case, the run is best placed next to the house where the window wall acts as one end of the run.

Runs that are not attached to the house are not as easily accessible for the cat. An isolated run means that the cat will have to rely on its owner to allow access to and from the run. In such circumstances, where a cat cannot gain easy access to the house, it is advisable to install a shelter within the run to cope with all weather conditions.

Will offering a cat run help to stop my cat from straying?

Installing a cat run will both protect a cat and prevent straying. Some adventurous cats will find the restrictions of the run frustrating, but the safety and health-protection factors vastly outweigh the lack of freedom.

Can I build a cat run myself?

It is perfectly straightforward to build a home-made run. You will need to be a practical person and have access to the necessary tools and materials. Most owners find it easier to ask a local joiner to construct the panels, leaving the bolting together as the only task.

What materials do I need to build a cat run?

A cat run is constructed from panels. These are made from wooden or PVC slats or lengths and fine-meshed wire.

The size of the panels is established in advance, from a plan based on how the final construction would best suit a particular home and garden.

Each wood or PVC frame should be a minimum of 2 m (6 ft 6 in) high, to allow you to stand inside the run. The width is usually about 1 m (3 ft 3 in), although larger widths can be achieved by using a stronger frame. The roof panels can be larger without having to resort to heavier-gauge wood or PVC frames, because they rely on the vertical sections for support. One section should include a door panel and lock to enable you to enter and leave. Each finished section is bolted securely to the next as the run is assembled.

It is possible to buy suitable panels by mail order through advertisements in specialist cat magazines or via the internet. If you are not able to assemble and erect the panels yourself, you can arrange for a joiner to do so on site.

Is it safe to use wood treatments?

A wood treatment will be necessary in order to protect wood-framed panels against the weather. There are many wood stains available that are environmentally friendly, and once dry they are guaranteed not to harm pets.

If you are not not sure about the status of a particular wood stain or preservative, ask at the DIY store or, better still, contact the manufacturers. It is better to do this before purchasing a wood preservative or stain, rather than checking afterwards only to find that the product is not appropriate for use on items to which pets will have access.

What should I put inside my cat run to make it an ideal environment for my cat?

There are a number of items that can be included in a cat run. Some of these are essential, others optional extras.

- An off-floor, raised box with a swing door will provide your cat with a dry, warm shelter and should be considered essential in any cat run.
- The most-used cat runs are those that provide many horizontal platforms or shelves for the cat to sit on, together with vertical sections to allow it the opportunity to climb. Make sure that platforms and shelves are made from sturdy materials and are properly fixed

in place, to prevent any potential collapse. An exploring pet could easily be injured in the confusion should a flimsy piece give way, especially under the greater weight of an adult cat.
- Grass should be included within the run floorspace if at all possible, as this is an important part of a cat's diet (see page 157). If the unit is set on concrete, this necessary 'green' patch can be provided easily by growing grass inside a trough within the run.
- Natural wood pieces, derived from logging of non-poisonous oak or beech trees, can put the finishing touches to a cat run. A sleeping cat, sprawled out on a tree trunk, can trigger visual echoes of wild felines in the jungle.

BELOW When you build your cat run, make sure that you only use wood preservatives and stains that are guaranteed pet safe.

Do I need to use a cattery when going away on holiday?

There are several cat-care options open to most cat owners who are going on holiday. The use of a cattery is the easiest and most convenient of these.

Some cats find life in the cattery nothing to be concerned about, and over a sequence of several visits will show few and decreasing signs of being unsettled or stressed by the temporary experience.

Others – especially cats of a nervous disposition or those that have developed a powerful attachment to their owners – may react badly to a stay in the cattery. This is because they are away from their normal territory and familiar home surroundings, and are separated from their owners.

If a cat has been boarded out early in life as a kitten or young adult, it will usually adapt to the changes knowing, or having learned, that the separation from you while in the cattery is only temporary and that you will return. For you, the owner, placing your cat in a cattery means you can relax in the knowledge that it will be fed, safe, secure and well cared for in your absence.

BELOW **Cats whose owners introduce them to a boarding cattery at an early age usually adapt quite easily to later visits.**

ABOVE **Always secure your cat in its carrier when you are taking it on a car journey or on public transport.**

How does my cat 'feel' when I leave it in a cattery?

It can be difficult not to be subjective about or to humanize a cat's emotional response to being left in a cattery. But cats view the world in an entirely different way to us.

Litter mothers move kittens from one site to another and leave them alone while hunting. The kittens have an innate or genetic understanding that the litter mother will make this decision and that it is necessary. The owner represents either a 'replacement litter mother' or a 'lead cat' and, as such, the decision to be

temporarily abandoned has to be accepted by the cat. It may be the cat's perception that its owner has gone 'hunting and foraging' and will return (as they usually do) with a 'kill' – neatly packaged in a tin!

If a cat is strongly bonded with or hyper-attached to its owner, then there would undoubtedly be some disorientation and perhaps mutual concern at the moment of separation. These cats will call or cry loudly for a short period before they withdraw and wait quietly for their owner's return.

Once they are taken back to their home and their usual environment, most cats will begin a brisk programme of re-scenting their owner, other members of the family and objects within the home by vigorously brushing up against them. This is the cat rightfully reclaiming what belongs to it. The episode in the cattery will soon be forgotten during this process of re-establishing the cat's place in the home.

Will it help if I give my cat its toys and bedding to have in the cattery?

The greatest disturbance to your cat's well-being will be caused by transporting it to another location and during the first moments of separation until it adjusts to your absence. It is possible to make separation more comfortable for a cat by supplying its normal bedding and a worn, throwaway item of its owner's clothing which carries your scent to act as a 'security blanket'.

Can I take my cat on holiday with me?

It is possible to take a house cat on holiday within the same country, provided that the hotel or other accommodation allows this. Special listing guides are available, but it is always wise to obtain verbal or even written confirmation that an establishment currently accepts pets.

Travel crates or cat carriers are ideal for taking your cat on car and train journeys, as well as for stays in hotels, cottages, caravans and on narrowboats. This is because, when used alongside a house litter tray, a part of a cat's inner home territory goes on holiday too! Using a carrier means you can be secure in the knowledge that the cat cannot bolt in a strange holiday location. Otherwise, an open car door can provide an unfortunate opportunity for the cat to panic, slip loose, run off, and quickly become disorientated, lost or, even worse, hurt.

A holiday abroad is more complicated with a cat. This would involve not only microchipping your cat but also extra vaccinations and several veterinary examinations. Some countries may even exclude cats and forbid their transfer between borders. It is best to always check at least six months in advance.

OPPOSITE It's important to start young in order to get a cat used to the cattery environment and being separated from its owner. Taking your cat's bedding, food and water bowls and some favourite toys will help to make it feel at home.

Does my cat need to have vaccinations and have been wormed to stay in a cattery?

All reputable catteries ask for a veterinary vaccination certification. This is to confirm that all visiting cats have been fully protected against known diseases. Worming will ensure that your cat is free from internal parasites.

How can I get my wary cat into the cat carrier?

It can be difficult to encourage a wary or wily cat into a carrier when it has a negative association with journeys to the veterinary surgeon. There are some steps you can take to make success more likely:

- Allow at least an hour before the journey, as you do not want to be rushing or stressing the cat.
- Use a strong cardboard box to encourage your cat to play hide and seek. If and when the cat enters the box, pick it up and transfer the now happier cat to the more appropriate carrier.
- When your cat is a kitten, reward it with food treats when it is in the carrier, to try to create a positive association with it.

Is it a good idea to use a cat sitter instead of a cattery?

In some regions there may be the option of a reputable local agency that can provide a trustworthy home pet sitter. Another variation on this that may be advertised in veterinary surgeries, pet magazines or on the internet is where a cat can live in a 'family home' via a service that offers a short-term, personal pet-sitting service.

Can I just ask a friend to come into my home and feed my cat?

You can avoid having to board your pet by asking a family member, friendly neighbour or friend to act as a 'sitter' for the holiday period. This is a good idea, because research suggests that cats (and dogs) prefer to remain in the place they know and in which they feel secure. However, it is important to ask helpers not to fuss a cat too much, and remember to leave them with a strict timetable of feeding, general instructions and your veterinary surgeon's contact details. A further alternative is for your cat to stay at a family member's or friend's home.

Can I use automatic feeders and water fillers while I am away?

House cats can safely be left at home for short periods using these devices. You will need to supply your cat with an automatic timer-feeder, an automatic water-bowl filler and a covered litter tray.

Should I do anything before I leave my cat?

It is best to adopt a 'no fuss, no emotion' and 'no eye contact' strategy during the

transfer. Otherwise, these human responses can transmit your anxieties directly to your pet. Try to organize the necessary paperwork beforehand, so that you can make a fast getaway. It is a mistake to cuddle your cat and tell it that you will be back soon, as this will simply cause it confusion.

Will my cat miss me?

Cats certainly 'miss' their owners when left. However, many quickly settle down into the fuss-free structure that is normally operated in professional cat-boarding facilities. The degree of problem related to separation is often dependent on the age of the cat and how attached it is to its owner. Few cats put on weight during the separation period, due to a combination of an appetite that is understandably reduced, less exercise and potentially varying degrees of withdrawn behaviour. However, if current veterinary records with regard to pet obesity are anything to go by, for many cats a little dieting wouldn't go amiss!

Can I bring a cat home from my holiday abroad?

Different countries have different rules about bringing an animal into a home country. The risk of introducing rabies and other exotic diseases means that veterinary examination and quarantine periods are necessary. A cat would become extremely stressed during the transfer and would certainly suffer through the subsequent quarantine boarding period. It is worth considering these aspects, together with the potentially high costs, before bringing a cat home from another country.

How should I behave towards my cat on my return?

It is always best to be calm and unfussy. The less fuss made towards a cat that has been concerned about its owner's absence, the sooner it will settle back into the normal routine. In the cat's mind, its owner has probably simply been away 'hunting for food'.

Why is my cat behaving aggressively on my return from holiday?

An owner's absence may frustrate a cat that has developed a powerful attachment to them. This may be triggered by the cat's failure to control its

owner's comings and goings in the way it wants. Frustration can lead to aggression (think road rage), and the cat then discharges its frustration by swiping at the person who it actually adores.

Why is my cat behaving nervously on my return from holiday?

The unexpected absence of an owner can sometimes lead a nervous cat to become even more anxious. It is, after all, impossible to explain in feline language that a holiday is about to occur. It is important not to fuss the cat and to ensure that everything gets back to the normal routine as soon as possible. Cats, like some people, find consistency and routine reassuring.

BELOW It is always advisable to consider the costs and trauma involved in bringing a cat home from another country.

Feeding
Your Cat

Can my cat eat the same food that I eat?

In theory, yes, although some foods intended for human consumption are not suitable. Your cat would probably refuse these anyway. Cat foods have been specifically developed by the major pet food manufacturers, who spend a great deal of time and money on research in order to ensure that the recipes sold offer a cat the ideal, balanced diet.

Cats need a meat-based (carnivorous) diet, as their natural prey consists of small mammals such as birds and rodents. Wild cats also actively seek out invertebrates such as insects, because these offer additional dietary input.

What is the best type of food for my cat?

Owners of today's domesticated cats have never had so much choice of foods to feed their pets. There are dried, tinned, semi-moist and fresh foods,

together with a wide range of tasty food treats ranging from freeze-dried to fresh prawns, tuna and all types of meat. All of these foods have something to offer a healthy, active cat.

Low-cost foods may not contain the ideal balance between proteins, carbohydrates, bulk, vitamins and minerals, but they can sustain a cat. More expensive foods may offer the ideal dietary balance and the price usually generally indicates the amount of research and development that has gone into the product, as well as the freshness of the ingredients.

Is it a good idea to vary my cat's diet?

Cats thrive on variety and naturally enjoy a change in both food type and texture. There are many recipes and types of food for cats available, in several forms from moist to dried.

The balance between proteins and carbohydrates in the food should reflect the age and activity level of the cat and many foods are marketed giving the suitable age. A young cat, aged between 3 and 12 months, is continually growing and would need a high level of protein for ideal growth and development. A cat of that age is usually very active and will 'burn up' the carbohydrates in proportion to the energy used, especially if it is an

LEFT Dried food contains the correct blend of ingredients, including vitamins and minerals, to sustain a healthy cat.

RIGHT If you can vary the place where you feed your cats it will help to stimulate their natural foraging skills.

outdoor type. Older cats should be offered low-protein foods or special diets for infirm cats, under veterinary guidance, but can still enjoy variety through the wide range of recipes available.

Can my cat eat some of my food scraps?

There is really only one reason why owners should be wary of offering a cat human food scraps. This is because a lot of human food contains a 'taste enhancer' such as sugar or salt that could disturb the cat's gastric balance, to the detriment of the cat. Some meats and poultry are high in protein, and if offered in large quantities can lead to stomach upsets.

It is possible to offer small scraps of food as special treats in foraging games or as rewards for good behaviour.

How often should I feed my cat?

Cats thrive on frequent meals. With the introduction of complete dried foods that stay fresh, you can offer your cat the opportunity to eat 24 hours a day. However, it is best to offer small, regular meals provided over the day and evening in order to keep a cat inquisitive and enthusiastic about its food.

Do I need special feed bowls for my cat?

It is a good idea to use purpose-made cat bowls that can be identified by the cat, and kept clean and in use. It is important that bowls are weighted to prevent them from travelling around the floor when the cat is feeding. Although side plates can be used to offer food to a cat, it is best to use a heavy, but shallow, porcelain or china bowl.

Where should I feed my cat?

It seems logical to offer a cat food in the same place all the time. Many owners place the food and water bowls on the same feeding mat, which is left permanently in position, but in fact it is useful to provide alternatives. If you can supervise, it is a good idea to move the food bowl around so that the cat has to seek it out, thereby encouraging its natural hunting instincts.

How much should I feed my cat?

The amount of food a cat should be given is usually indicated on the tin or packet. However, some greedy cats would eat the whole tin if given the chance. It is best not to offer too much food at each meal otherwise the cat will become fat. Provided a sensible amount of food is given, it is best to offer several smaller meals rather than a single large bowl of food.

Do I need to give my cat vitamin and mineral supplements?

If a cat is offered a healthy, balanced diet, including complete cat food and fresh foods, this will normally provide all the vitamins and minerals it needs. Nevertheless, there are occasions when a cat is physically and mentally stressed – perhaps when recovering from injury or intrusive surgery, or when a litter mother

FEEDING GUIDE FOR ADULT CATS

Age	Frequency	Food
9–12 months	2–3 meals daily	1 titbit, 1 dry, 1 moist
12–36 months	Active cat: 2–3 meals daily	Active cat: 1 titbit, 1 dry, 1 moist
	Indoor, less active cat: 2 meals daily	Indoor, less active cat: 1 dry, 1 semi-moist or titbit
3–5 years	Active cat: 2 meals daily	Active cat: 1 dry, 1 semi-moist or titbits
	Indoor, less active cat: 1 meal daily	Indoor, less active cat: complete dry food with small amounts of titbit treats
5 years +	Active cat: 2 meals daily	Active cat: 1 complete dry or semi-moist, 1 titbit
	Indoor, less active cat: 1 meal daily	Indoor, less active cat: complete dry 'mature cat' food, occasional titbit treats

Note A titbit meal or treat can consist of strips of fresh or lightly blanched fish, microwaved fatty mincemeat or semi-moist food.

is pregnant or in post-natal recovery. At these times the cat's immune system will be under pressure, and it would be sensible to add supplements to the diet. Consult your veterinary practice for advice.

Does my cat need milk?

There has been much debate around this question. Mammal milk is species-specific and some researchers involved in nutrition and allergies would argue that it is not wise to give one animal's milk to another. The fact that cats readily lap up cow's milk is not a scientific argument that it is good for them. Others argue that there are ingredients in milk which offer much-needed calcium and fats, but in fact these important nutrients could easily be offered in other ways.

Why does my cat not like water fresh from the tap?

The antibacterial additives in fresh tap water probably taste unappetizing and alien to a cat. Chlorine and phenols in water will taste particularly strong to felines. Standing water, such as that in a toilet bowl, has usually become free of chlorine because it naturally dissipates as oxygen leaves when the water warms to room temperature. A cat may then try to drink it.

RIGHT Cats will actively seek out water that is free of chemicals. They know by instinct that it enhances their digestive processes.

Why do cats drink dirty water?

Cats actively seek out water that is 'organic' – free of the chemicals used to treat tap water. This is because they know instinctively that the bacterial content will enhance gastric digestion.

Why do some cats drink from a dripping tap?

It is thought that cats are attracted to the movement – of both the water and the light that is reflected and refracted. Many cats attempt to catch the light and

in doing so they wet their paws. It is then natural for the cat to lick its paws clean. Cats may also be attracted to and enjoy the sound of the water dripping.

ABOVE Cats are attracted to moving water and the light reflected in it such as the water from a running tap.

Why is my cat fussy about food?

Cats have an innate evolutionary desire to vary their diet. This behavioural mechanism may have developed to protect them against missing out on a number of vitamins and minerals that

may not be accessed if small mammals or rodents are their only prey.

Wild cats would target a number of invertebrates, including a wide range of insects, grubs and worms, in order to supplement their natural diet. In domesticated cats, this behaviour is paralleled by seeking out changes in regular foods.

RIGHT When they are sufficiently full, cats will leave amounts of food, especially in the absence of any competition.

Why does my cat go off a certain food and then seem to thrive on a change?

Because cats naturally look for diversity in food (see left), they often reject a favourite dish for another. You can use this to advantage, by rotating certain food types to encourage appetite and help to deal with a cat's apparent lack of interest in its regular food.

Should I leave food out all the time?

Most owners are happy to leave dried food out on a permanent basis. However, this can lead to food predictability and boredom. It is a good idea to use food to stimulate a house cat, by hiding it (see page 132) or by offering a total amount of food each day at various times (not in a set pattern) spread through the day.

Why does my cat not like food that has been kept in the fridge?

Cats prefer food to be 'kill warm'. Coldness indicates long-dead food that only a starving hunter-scavenger would consider. Prepared food that has been refrigerated should be removed and brought to room temperature in a secure place. Do not return uneaten food to the refrigerator.

Why does my cat leave part of its food for a day or more?

Cats may sometimes express a form of possession by leaving a certain amount of their food. They can also learn that no other competitor is going to take the food that has been left and then remember that it is safe to do so.

ABOVE **Active and owner-interactive cats often demand additional food but it is not sensible to overfeed a housebound cat.**

Do I need to throw away food that is over a day old?

Complete dried food can be offered over a period of several days. Fresh, tinned or semi-moist packaged foods should be disposed of after a day, as they can introduce unwanted bacteria into a cat's digestive system.

My cat eats all his food and then looks for more. Does this mean he's greedy?

Some active cats have a powerful appetite that develops from their need to fuel their exercise. Looking for more food is acceptable in this instance – it can be useful to leave such a cat wanting more, to enable food to be used for interaction and hunting games. However, it is not advisable to over-feed a house-bound cat, as an adult cat can quickly become overweight and this can lead to health problems.

Are prepared foods best for cats?

In the early development of canned foods, valuable vitamins and minerals could be lost or degraded in the high water content. Now, manufacturers have found better ways to stabilize the additives and other contents. Many cats thrive perfectly happily on a diet of prepared foods, but some lose interest and will then need to be offered a variation in food types and textures to tempt them into eating again.

DRIED FOODS

Advantages	Disadvantages
Valuable vitamins and minerals are stabilized.	Makes for a somewhat predictable diet.
Contents do not deteriorate as quickly as with tinned or fresh food.	Additives and taste enhancers have to be added to make it more attractive to cats.
Quantities can be accurately measured out with no left-overs in the fridge.	Cat will need access to more water and will then urinate more.
Food can be left in the bowl for the cat to eat as and when it requires.	
Crisp texture can help to keep the cat's teeth free from plaque.	
Storage life and weight-to-cost ratio compare extremely well with canned and semi-moist foods.	

What are the advantages and disadvantages of dried food?

The development of 'complete' dried foods has revolutionized how cat owners feed their pets. The advantages and disadvantages are summarized in the table above.

Are semi-moist foods best for cats?

Semi-moist foods represent a 'halfway house'. They offer a fresher variation on tinned foods, and an alternative to a diet based solely on dried food. With small packets and variations in recipes, it is possible to offer a cat an interesting and healthy diet. The higher cost of this type of food should be considered by owners who have a fixed budget for their pet.

Do I need to offer my cat fresh foods?

It is healthy and satisfying to the cat, to offer a wide range of food types. When offering fresh foods, there are some guidelines to follow:
• Do not over-cook or over-feed any fresh food such as fish, mincemeat or

ABOVE **Cats need variety in their food. Fish, meat and poultry can be supplemented by vegetables and cereals.**

portions of daily food or special food treats. Place measured amounts of food into fairy (cup) cake papers or even packets (nothing that is too difficult to open). Identify an appropriate area in the house in which to hide at least half and perhaps all of the normal food ration. The cat then has to use its natural abilities to track down and locate the hidden food.

poultry. Over-cooking leads to some loss of taste and nutrients, while over-feeding can reduce the cat's appetite for standard foods.

- Small strips of fish or mincemeat should be blanched or lightly microwaved so that the food is 'kill warm'.
- Small pieces of chicken must be fully cooked, to prevent the possible transfer of salmonella.
- Before offering a cat fresh foods of this type, remember that they are all high in protein and should not be fed in large quantities. This applies to older cats in particular.

Can I make food and feeding interesting for my cat?

You can do this by occasionally turning feeding into a game. Instead of simply offering your cat its food in a bowl, organize a hide-and-seek game with

Why does my cat hunt birds and mice even though he is well-fed?

Regular meals actually ensure that the cat has the health, strength and energy to hunt down prey. If a farmer or warehouseman wants to encourage the natural hunting skills of a working cat, the advice is that he should feed up the cat first. A well-fed cat can busy itself stalking, hunting and locating prey for long periods. The house cat in this situation does not need the prey as a food item and will often bring back the trophy – in some cases, alive – to 'share' with its owner.

How can I stop my cat bringing home prey?

Outdoor 'hunter' cats target small birds, rodents, insects and even juvenile rabbits. This instinctive hunting behaviour, which persists even though the cat is well-fed, can be extremely difficult to eradicate as it is a natural instinct for a cat. It is possible to add a warning bell on the collar or to use a sonic unit that will alert potential prey and reduce successful strike rates.

How often should I clean out my cat's bowls?

You should clean out your cat's feed bowl and rinse it in warm water on a daily basis. Cats are clean animals and can appear almost phobic about odours that suggest food has deteriorated. Water bowls should be cleaned out every few days, depending on the quantity of water that the cat has consumed.

What should I use to clean out my cat's bowls?

Bowls that are cleaned out on a daily basis will not become encrusted with traces of uneaten food. A daily warm water rinse, plus a weekly wash with soap, is all that should be required. Any residue from strong-smelling detergents can cause a cat to decline its food, so these should be avoided.

BELOW Extremely active, hunter cats will bring prey home, but a warning bell on their collars can help to alert potential prey.

How can I tell if my cat is overweight?

The best method is to ask a veterinary nurse to weigh your cat at its annual health check. This will give you a professional opinion based on the cat's age, size and gender. A cat that looks like a fur balloon is obviously overweight, but it is important to prevent obesity before any serious side effects, such as breathing difficulties, heart problems or arthritis, occur. Comparing your cat with a photograph from a couple of years ago can tell you if it has put on weight.

ABOVE Obesity is not just a problem for humans. Fat cats also run the risk of health problems resulting from obesity.

How can I tell if my cat is underweight?

As with the overweight cat (see left), have your cat's weight checked during its routine health check or when vaccinations are given. In this way, all factors can be taken into consideration by a professional. An active cat will often be lean, as this adds to its stealth factor.

Can a happy cat be 'too fat'?

Stereotypically, fat cats are thought to be happy and contented. To some extent it is true that a contented cat will naturally put on weight, because it is often home-loving and only too pleased to avoid the rigours of outdoors for the safety, comfort and owner-love that the house represents. However, an overweight cat is vulnerable to major organ failure and possible bone and muscle deterioration, due to the extra body-stress that extra weight causes. Obesity can therefore reduce lifespan.

Can I put my overweight cat on a diet?

It is possible to cut down on the amount of food given to an overweight cat. However, you should also discuss the situation with a veterinary surgeon or other professional within the clinic who has nutritional expertise. They may be able to suggest a feline health diet to support a controlled weight-reduction programme for your cat.

How can I get my cat to put on weight, and is weight-loss serious?

Encouraging a cat to eat more and run around less can be a challenge. Try playing hunting and locating games with food to make eating more attractive (see page 132) or offer food in a variety of recipes and textures to stimulate good eating habits.

At the first signs of visible weight loss, it is vital that your veterinary surgeon performs a feline health check. If the possible physical factors, such as blood diseases, tooth and gum conditions and digestion problems are eliminated, then it would be useful to discuss your cat's condition urgently with a cat behaviourist to explore the possibilities for 'curing' its lack of appetite.

Why does my cat display excessive flatulence and is this diet-related?

There are some foods that, when combined with digestive imbalances, can encourage gases to build up in a cat's stomach. This situation could lead to excessive and unpleasant flatulence that persists over a period of time. Long-haired cats that suffer from fur-ball problems (see page 222) may also experience excessive wind and should be examined by a vet.

What diet should I give my older cat?

Older cats are no longer growing and are likely to be less active than younger ones. Because of this, they do not require high levels of protein in their food. For these cats, and those that are housebound, seek out a food designed for older cats and keep each meal modest in size. A housebound cat would not normally be as active as would an outdoor cat and therefore would need less food.

7

Cat Behaviour

How does my cat *really* view me?

When a kitten is first separated from its litter mother and siblings, plus any associated humans, there is much for it to adapt to and learn about. The owner is sniffed as they undertake the human stroking and petting ritual, in order to ascertain who that person is. The human scents that the cat smells will offer information about gender through testosterone and oestrogen, and perhaps about dominant emotions from skin pheromones. A high proportion of a cat's information about its world is gained through scents and smells.

The new owner in effect becomes a 'replacement litter mother' or even a 'replacement lead cat' to the kitten, because all the normal functions of maternal behaviour are taken over by the human. These include:

ABOVE A kitten will potentially view its new owner as a replacement litter mother. Its point of view changes as it grows older.

- Exploring outside the 'nest area' (perhaps the bedroom).
- Providing the 'kill' (thanks to cat food manufacturers).
- Moving the kitten around.
- Protecting it from danger.

Eventually, the maturing cat would probably see its kind and non-aggressive owner as a 'replacement mate' and, potentially, their human partners as 'competitive males' or 'passive females'. This is likely to be the view from a cat's point of view.

The cat's brain does not include the equivalent of our frontal lobes. They cannot switch perspectives and see the world from our (intellectual and considerably elevated) viewpoint. They

ABOVE **Children probably represent both a threat and the promise of a playmate, depending on how they interact with a young kitten.**

make simple decisions based on their own instinctive responses and learned experiences, such as:

- Are we humans part of their social structure or not?
- Are we a threat or not?
- Are we predator or prey?

They cannot 'think' that we are cats and/or they are humans. That 'intelligent' perception is far too complicated for cats, however apparently clever they may appear. Even though we are biped to their quadruped, owners probably represent 'giant cats' because of the way we interact with them and act as natural replacements.

How do cats view children?

When sniffed at by cats, children may be seen as kittens or juvenile cats because of their lower hormone levels. If a child is particularly boisterous, they may be viewed as troublesome and to be avoided if at all possible. If children tease or mishandle a cat they may be seen as dangerous and to be avoided at all costs. This is learned behaviour among some worldly wise domesticated felines.

Some children have been known to form extremely strong bonds with their cats. The quality of attachment and relationship can often continue into adult life for both of them. A cat called Tabitha remained with her teenaged owner until she was an adult and moved to live away from her parents. At 16 years of age (over 80 years in human terms), the cat refused to accept her owner's new partner when he first arrived in her home. Eventually, with behavioural treatment, Tabitha relented and began to 'possess' him in the normal cat way.

How do cats view dogs?

This is no definitive answer to this. Some cats and dogs live together in harmony, some in discord. A recent case allowed the observation of a cat sitting on the dog as it lay on the sofa, grooming the canine's face – much to the pleasure of both parties. In other cases, cats have attacked the dog or the cat was pounced upon the moment it moved from underneath a chair.

Cats probably make simple decisions when checking out a dog:

BELOW As a fellow predator, a kitten probably views a dog as a threat. Whereas an adult cat, with experience and socialization, may not.

- Is the dog a threat or a non-threat?
- Is the dog part of the social group or outside it?
- Is it a predator to be feared or one to compete with for resources?

The degree of peace or hostility between a cat and a dog will often depend entirely on the temperament of both animals, and whether they have been socialized together as youngsters.

What do cats think of strangers in my home?

This depends on the temperament of the cat. A calm, contented cat will view a stranger entering the home as a non-threatening animal who is on the periphery of the social structure. From hormonal signals, the cat will know gender and probably whether the person is calm or anxious. A nervous cat will probably view the stranger as a threat and will immediately seek refuge in the nearest bolt hole.

Why does my cat run and hide when people come into my home?

This behaviour is about feline personality and temperament. A confident cat will want to investigate all of the 'animals' that enter its inner territory, represented by the home. The nervous cat will not want to deal with the potential threat and possible competition, and so will avoid confrontations of any kind by hiding elsewhere in the home.

Is it beneficial for my cat to be stroked?

Most cats appear to 'enjoy' being stroked by their owners. This apparent willingness on the part of cats to succumb to human needs suggests that there is a benefit to them in this behaviour. However, it is probably more accurate to analyse the interaction as the cat perceiving that the human is performing marking behaviour as they stroke the cat and, seemingly deliberately, leave their skin scent behind on it. Cats may not fight against being stroked (although some cats do shy away or become aggressive during interaction that involves stroking), and they may even thrive on the cross-marking behaviour. In this analysis, there would clearly be a benefit to being stroked, but it may not be equally balanced between human and cat.

Why is it said to be therapeutic to stroke a cat?

There is plenty of medical evidence to suggest that this is the case. When humans stroke their warm-blooded companion animals, there is a reduction in stress levels, heart rate and blood pressure levels. Cats can easily become the living equivalent of 'comfort blankets' to people because they are soft, warm and furry, and because the relationship would appear to be motivated by love alone.

The apparent altruism is not without ulterior motives on the part of the cats, however, because they clearly have feline

agendas that include 'possession', 'access to resources' (food, warmth and protection) and potential 'control' over the human-feline relationship. The unconditional aspect of loving a companion animal is probably that a cat will never 'inform' on its owner for any behaviour or tell another human being what has been said to it by the owner, and will never be judgemental.

Why does my cat not seem to enjoy being stroked?

Cats do not 'stroke' each other in the same way that humans do as part of our tactile, loving behaviour towards family members and close friends. Litter mothers and cats within a close social group do perform cleaning or grooming behaviours (allogrooming, see right) towards kittens or each other, but it is not the same as human behaviour.

Once domestication 'tamed' the wild cat, it soon learned to accept the human desire to stroke as part of the relationship. This is probably perceived initially by the cat as 'replacement mother' behaviour and eventually as 'marking' behaviour, because owners leave their scent on the cat when they are stroking them.

Certain cats may feel their owner is invading their body space and they react adversely to that aspect of stroking. Another reason why other cats shy away from being stroked may be that they are

OPPOSITE **Some cats will view the human behaviour of stroking as an invasion of body space.**

dominant in the relationship and are not willing to allow stroking behaviour because it may be seen as being 'subdominant' to the owner. Always stroke your cat in the direction of the fur and never push the whiskers forward.

Is it better to stroke each cat in turn?

This is fine when the cats are fully socialized and non-aggressive with each other. However, when there is some competition between cats – often when group stability has not been achieved, or if nervous adopted cats are kept together – stroking can increase their aggression towards each other. In basic terms, the owner transfers the scent from each cat to the next and it is this that can increase feline competitive behaviour. To play safe, owners should use their other hand to stroke the next cat and then wash their hands between stroking sessions to remove the cats' scents.

What is 'allogrooming'?

Cats that live in social groups perform mutual grooming and litter mothers perform reflex-period grooming of kittens before they are able to self-groom. This behaviour is known as allogrooming. The term can be used generally to describe maternal behaviour towards growing kittens, but is especially relevant to mutual grooming between adult cats where there is trust and confidence between them.

ABOVE A cat may be triggered into behaving aggressively in order to control interaction with humans.

Why do cats groom each other?

The exact purpose behind mutual grooming behaviour in cats is not fully understood. Adult cats can groom themselves perfectly well and therefore the behaviour must have its roots in the evolution of social behaviour in felines. In primate behaviour, allogrooming helps to reduce parasite infestations and there may be a similar link in cats. There is also an indication that there is some connection between feline allogrooming and sexual display, as most of the large male cats such as lions and tigers have been observed licking a female in a grooming style prior to copulation.

Why does my cat sit on my knee to be cuddled and then become aggressive?

Cats do not exactly 'cuddle' each other, although they might sometimes snuggle up together for mutual warmth and protection. Most companion cats want interaction with their owner, but some nervous or instinctive cats may wish to remain in control of the relationship. Once the interaction with the owner becomes superfluous to the cat's needs, then it will use an act of aggression to show a desire to break off the contact on its own terms. In this instance, a need to control the tentative harmony triggers an instinctive need to break off contact with the person, and violence expresses the cat's reaction to what it perceives as an invasion of its body space – in a similar way to humans not wanting an uninvited hug from another person.

Is it healthy for my cat to rest for most of the day?

It can do a cat no harm whatsoever to spend the day lazing around, dozing, yawning and then dozing again. In fact it is perfectly natural. Cats are fundamentally nocturnal animals and such creatures need to rest during daylight hours in order to build the strength and energy they need to perform their night-time activities.

BELOW Contented cats spend a great deal of time sleeping. A cat spends an average of 17 hours a day asleep.

How do cats learn to do 'clever things'?

Cats are extremely good at low-level problem-solving that requires learning by association. They may learn to perform behaviours through two different brain mechanisms:

1 Classical conditioning In this way of learning, the cat responds to a 'conditioned' stimulus (say, its owner opening a tin of food) and what follows is a 'natural' or 'unconditioned' stimulus (the smell of food) to give a 'conditioned' response (looking for food, meowing). The cat learns that by going to the cupboard where the cat food is and

vocalizing its desires it can trigger the owner to offer food.

2 Instrumental learning In this process, the cat works through a number of actions to, say, open a door. When it succeeds by jumping at the handle, this action is repeated because it is deemed both successful and rewarding. This is 'trial and error' learning.

These two defining ways of learning mean that the cat comes to understand that there is 'pleasure' to be obtained from performing a particular task and responding to a stimulus. This means that these behaviours will be repeated and the associations made and reinforced or promoted.

Are some cat breeds more nervous than others?

There is a myth that suggests pure pedigree cats, and in particular certain breeds such as the Siamese, are more sensitive than other cats. In fact, research has shown that pedigree cats experience roughly the same number of behavioural problems as non-pedigree cats.

It would actually be true to say that highly instinctive, often feral-influenced non-pedigree cats are more disposed to express nervous behaviours than are the ideally socialized offspring of contented house cats, whether the latter are pedigree or not.

OPPOSITE **Although we view a cat rubbing itself against our legs as a sign of welcome, it is actually their way of 'marking' us in a possessive way.**

Why does my cat ambush my feet as I walk through a room?

This is a cat performing behaviours that are instinctive. Feline play and predatory aggression are closely intertwined, and movement stimulates a 'motor reaction' signal in the cat's brain. The movement of your feet at the cat's eye level then triggers 'pounce and attack' behaviour, as they act as a replacement for the moving bird or mouse.

Why does my cat rub against my legs?

This is a feline behaviour that involves 'marking' and 'possession'. From a psychologist's point of view, one of the most interesting aspects of companion animal interaction is the 'crossed wires' that occur between humanization and felinization. The owner may see the cat's behaviour as friendly, because humans who are physically close with each other show love and affection by being tactile. The cat, on the other hand, may view the owner's willingness to be 'marked' and therefore 'possessed' as submissive and highly sociable.

Why does my cat immediately rub against visitors who come into our home?

A cat perceives any animal – including humans – entering its 'inner territory' as potential competition. Resources that may be under threat include food, relationships and territory. The cat's primary instinct is to investigate – scents that humans give off will inform the cat about gender and emotional state (see page 138) – 'mark' and 'possess' the human (see page 149). Once the behaviours have been performed and nothing untoward has happened during the interaction, then the cat will have been successful in marking and possessing the human and can then be content in that knowledge.

Why does my cat head-butt me and my hand?

Cats pass information to and communicate with each other in various ways. Body language, scenting and marking are probably the most important of these methods. All of these behaviours occur between the developing kittens and their litter mother as part of communication behaviour. In addition, cats being scent-marking machines from head to tail (see page 79), they use all parts of their bodies to communicate their desires, in order to interact with one another and to survive.

Head-butting among adult cats, which is also known as allorubbing, may facilitate the use of marking glands on the face that enable them to 'mark and possess' targets for this behaviour (see page 147). Some cats perform this behaviour more than others: research suggests that repeated head-butting of humans by a cat can be interpreted as an indication that the cat has a strong desire to control the relationship between itself and its owner.

Are cats sharpening their claws when they scratch on tree trunks, fences and posts?

It is extremely unlikely that a cat is testing out the sharpness of its claws when it begins scratching on an object. When cats perform scratching behaviour, they are bringing into use special scent glands to mark the target. All felines, including the big cats, will climb a tree trunk within a territory and use scent glands within their paws to mark it – this can extend to the highest point. Tigers have been observed with all four feet off the ground as they perform claw-marking behaviour on a tree trunk. This behaviour helps to pass on marking information about gender and oestrus onto competitors, other predators and potential sexual mates.

Can some cats 'talk'?

Cats do vocalize their intentions, albeit in a very basic way compared to our human vocabulary. Domesticated cats especially have learned to modify their greeting call, when a variation in the basic meow (which can include slight variations, depending on the country of origin) attracts the immediate attention of an owner. The cat soon makes the connection between the modification of its greeting call and the speed of response from the owner. The 'rewards' for learning this may be instant access to food, contact with the owner or access to other territories beyond the home.

Owners believe that some cat breeds, such as the Siamese, are very vocal, but

ABOVE **Scent glands within the paws enable cats to mark when they scratch and to pass on information to other cats.**

excessive vocalization can often be linked to mutual over-dependency between cat and owner. It could be that Siamese cats have a predisposition to interact more with owners and have learned to do so, then this behaviour is passed on to the kittens.

Why does my cat purr?

Research suggests that purring is for communication. It is exclusive to cats as a group and is not simply a behaviour encouraged in domestication to enhance the feline-human relationship.

Kittens naturally purr – in the reflex period when they are blind (see page 205). This may enable the litter mother to locate them faster when they become separated. Kittens purr when they are

being groomed, before, during or immediately after sleeping, or preceding and following a feeding session with the litter mother.

Purring can occur in adult cats, both wild and domesticated, in the following circumstances:
- When the cat is experiencing pain, when it is seen as a counter-stress development.
- During displays of aggression.
- During sexual behaviour.

This unique feline vocalization occurs more in domesticated cats than in their wild cousins, and is seen (when humanized) as a sign of contentment in companion cats. Adult cats often begin to purr when they perceive themselves as safe and secure, and while they are enjoying social interaction and contact with their owners.

The sound and vibration that are associated with purring are created somewhere between the chest cavity and the throat area known as the glottis, and is controlled by pulse-contracting laryngeal muscles. The true nature of how purring is created and its function are still being researched. There are various contradictory theories, but it is undoubtedly fascinating to recognize that the sound is not simply a result of the cat using its vocal chords. One theory about the development of purring is that sounds that involve strong vibrations are particularly effective at night.

OPPOSITE **Cats learn how to interact with their owners by vocalizing aspects of their needs, frustration and security.**

Why does my cat hiss and spit?

Cats have developed this method of communicating their dislike for a potential competitor or a feared predator. It is similar to the way a human audience will boo and hiss at the pantomime villain. Cats use hissing in an attempt both to warn and to discourage further approach from a human stranger or another pet, potential feline competitor or feared predator. This form of feline communication developed as a means of avoiding an act of aggression, such as a fight with another cat or an attack from a predator, that could result in physical injuries. In nature, it is always preferable to avoid conflicts, as a serious injury can result in fatality.

Why does my cat only hiss and spit at certain people, or particular cats and dogs?

A cat will make an assessment on the potential threat posed by an approaching animal, be it human, feline or canine. If it perceives itself to be at risk, the cat has to react with either fight or flight.

Once a cat has made a negative association with a competitor or other animal, it needs to advise them that an encounter could result in its aggression. To avoid the actual act of aggression at all costs, a cat creates the strongest emotion by hissing and spitting. Hopefully, the target for this form of communication will take heed and promptly leave the scene before a potential fight can occur.

Why does my cat meow?

The cat's meow is its primary calling method for obtaining attention. There are slight variations in the sound, depending on the cat's country of origin. Meowing will be directed first at the litter mother, and then later at a 'lead cat' or owner. Litter mothers often move kittens from one place to another in the early days for safety reasons, and the meow will sometimes help her to locate them. Developing kittens learn to use the call and modify its length in order to communicate urgency or to beg for their share of the kill. Adult cats in social groups may use the call in order to be allowed close contact or to share food.

Why does my cat cry?

A kitten or adult cat quickly learns that a cry (higher pitched than a meow) can elicit a faster response from an owner. A cry is a passive form of vocalization that between cats would indicate submission or injury. Cats that have developed an over-dependent relationship with concerned owners will use a cry to gain urgent contact, food, or entry to and exit from the home. They may repeat the call over and over again until it is successful.

Why does my cat yowl?

'Yowling' or 'caterwauling' is a mating call associated with non-spayed queens that are interested in sexual activity. Sometimes entire toms may join in such a night-time chorus, but they might also be busy hissing and spitting to help keep competitive males away.

Nocturnal animals often need to communicate their desires to one another in the vocal way that birds sing and primates call. Sound travels further under the cover of darkness, enabling the yowl to project over a wider area. A cat that is ready for mating can use this distinctive sound to help lure potential mates closer to it, until pheromones (sexual body scents) can do the rest.

LEFT **Cats naturally seek out warm, enclosed spaces in the home.**

OPPOSITE **Cats will climb to an elevated position when they are hunting or escaping a predator.**

Can cats growl like dogs?

Males cats can create a low growling sound and often do this when competing males are around. It is thought that the growl, being the lowest-pitched sound a cat can produce, enables it to communicate dominance. The growl form of feline communication is common among the big cats, and it is believed that by producing deep growls small cats may deceive potential competitors into perceiving them to be larger and therefore more dangerous as opponents than they really are.

Why does my cat hide in a cupboard?

Cats feel more secure in concealed dens or bolt holes. In nature, bolt holes might be folds in the undergrowth, spaces

between boulders, holes in tree trunks or burrows. When concealed in a narrow space, a cat is protected from potential threats and predators, both on the ground and from the air and so feels secure. For domesticated cats, the home cupboard is a handy replacement.

Why does my cat like to hide in high places?

Cats in nature have learned the advantages of an elevated position over millions of years. It is ideal for surveying for ground-based and flighted prey, and also offers a place of safety from large terrestrial predators.

When house cats are under competitive pressure from others or perceive that there are dangers within their territory, they will often seek out an elevated position up a tree, on a wall or on a roof.

Cats apparently stuck in trees usually are not. They have often been pursued by other cats or chased by dogs, and in the panic to survive have taken refuge in the highest position they can find. The cat will often choose the least safe branch in terms of the weight that it will take: this strategy means that the chasing animal has to calculate the cost of aggression against the risk to its own safety. In this situation, the cat is under great stress and its adrenalin levels will be high, to enhance its 'flight or fight' behaviours. Once the cat deems itself to be no longer under threat and adrenalin levels have subsided naturally, it will often be perfectly able to back down the tree slowly and carefully.

Why does my cat bring prey it has killed to me?

Once kittens are on solid food, the litter mother will carry prey back to them on a daily basis throughout her care period. In the absence of a litter to feed, a cat with a hunting personality will use this instinctive behaviour to bring home prey that it rarely needs for itself. Healthy feeding cats have more than enough energy to hunt and seem to enjoy bringing back 'trophies' that help to show off their skill and healthiness.

Fundamentally, your cat wants to share its kill with you just as you share yours (cat food, treats and human food) with it. The cat's kill might be a young rabbit, bird or a mouse, but it is not really any different to what you offer your cat – just without the packaging.

Why does my cat bring prey home alive?

Litter mothers bring prey back alive for maturing kittens, so that they can practise how to kill through play. Dead prey will obviously not help them in this respect. As cats mature, they need to learn how to identify and locate prey,

and make a quick kill. The latter is especially important, as vital energy can be lost if there is a prolonged struggle between a young feline predator and the prey. All in all, kittens can learn a great deal from live prey.

Adult cats often confuse this need for kittens to learn with a perceived similar need in their owners. Although it is not advisable on health and ethical grounds, an owner could simply attack and bite the prey in the neck in true 'predatory' fashion, and carry it off to the kitchen. Perhaps only then will the deluded cat be satisfied.

RIGHT Hunting is instinctive behaviour for cats. A young cat may play with prey or bring it home to share the kill with its owner.

OPPOSITE Some cats have a strong hunting instinct especially, paradoxically, when they are healthy and well nourished.

ABOVE Cats, especially long-haired ones, will eat grass to help them regurgitate ingested fur. House-bound cats will appreciate a small box of grass.

Are there any positive steps I can take to reduce my cat's need to hunt live prey?

Some cats are true hunters – and they are often the better-fed ones. A healthy, well-nourished cat has the energy to direct into stalking, prowling, pouncing and leaping at the small mammals that would be its normal diet in nature. A wild cat spends a huge amount of its time hunting and catching prey, and yet in domestication they usually receive their food without any effort on their part. Nevertheless, there are some steps you can take to prevent them:

ABOVE Cats, especially long-haired ones, will eat grass to help them regurgitate ingested fur. House-bound cats will appreciate a small box of grass.

- Attach a warning bell to the cat's collar or there are sonic collar units on the market that can alert potential prey of a cat's approach and therefore reduce its strike rate.
- Harness your cat's natural hunting desires by regularly playing hide-and-seek games with morsels of especially delicious food. Create little rice-paper parcels of prawns, lightly microwaved minced meat (rare, not fully cooked)

and slivers of fish. These can be hung from banister rails or doors, or dragged along on pieces of string. The small parcels of food can be hung up or hidden around the home and left behind when the family is out, and the cat will enjoy tracking them down and eating them. When the cat has used up enough physical and mental energy on a daily basis, it should tire of real hunting.

How do I stop my cat from wandering off for days on end?

It is in the nature of some cats to enjoy exploring and hunting. Some are so absorbed in what they are doing that they lose track of both time and their territory. It is difficult to counter such a feline temperament.

There is also a condition in cats that develops into 'detached' behaviour where they do not want to 'belong' to one particular home. These cats will find a warm place and some food from kind neighbours or even in homes that are miles away from the cat's normal territorial range.

It is possible to counter wandering and detached behaviour in cats by enhancing the home environment. This could include:
- Installing tall scratching posts in the home and spraying them with catnip (see page 178–179).
- Playing lure games with a 'fishing rod', where a food treat is attached to a line to be flicked away and drawn along to encourage a chase.

- Feeding at varied times rather than just leaving food down in a dish for the cat to consume when it feels the need.

These strategies will help to make the cat feel more interested in and therefore more attached to its home.

What should I do now my cat has gone missing for more than a day?

Most owners will fear the worst, but it is often just a case of feline adventure taking priority over home life. Sometimes, a missing pet will have found itself vigorously pursued by a very aggressive or amorous cat, and in these circumstances can quite easily become disorientated and confused. This stressed state may initially affect its normal ability to find its way back home to its own established territory.

Unless it is completely out of character for a cat to be away for more than a day, it is best to remain calm and await its return. If, on the other hand, you are particularly anxious and concerned you can initiate a search (see page 68).

Is it all right for my cat to eat grass?

Cats naturally nibble grass to aid regurgitation of fur. They may also benefit from small amounts in their diet. For indoor cats or those that are restricted to a run, it is possible to grow several troughs of grass that can be rotated between uses.

Why does my cat catch and eat spiders and flies?

It is quite natural for a cat to catch and eat invertebrates. These creatures are part of a cat's normal diet in the wild. Insects adds variety to the cat's diet of small mammals such as birds and mice, and also provide the cat with important vitamins, minerals and chitin (fingernail-like material). These are a good dietary addition, because they are essential for the development of claws and whiskers, enhancing their strength and growth.

Why does my cat repeatedly prod my cardigan with its paws?

This juvenile behaviour is linked to kittens feeding on the litter mother's teats. It can also be displayed in adult cats that have been removed from the litter mother before the normal 10 weeks of close maternal care is finished. The alternate paw prodding appears to calm the cat and may be a stress reducer, with the adult cat possibly becoming addicted to its effects.

Why does my cat like to lick me?

A cat uses scents and smells like humans use conversation. Felines can glean a great deal of information by licking and they may also obtain salts from a person's skin. In addition, there is an element of 'displaced allogrooming behaviour' – the mutual grooming that might occur between sociable cats (see page 143) but becomes transferred to the owner. Some cats can become obsessed with licking and grooming because of the calming effect of repeated ('stereotypical') behaviour (see below).

Why does my cat frequently lick itself?

Cats love to groom themselves. A groomed fur coat and clean whiskers and paws can enhance a hunter's ability to stalk in the shadows and undergrowth and surprise unsuspecting prey. However, grooming can become obsessive and compulsive in some cats that are suffering the effects of stress. Causes of stress include competition between home cats, aggression from neighbouring feral cats and trauma (see page 213).

Why is my cat creating bald patches on his coat?

If there is no dermatological cause for the hair loss (consult your veterinary surgeon), then this is often a sign of feline stress. When a cat is suffering the effects of stress it often begins grooming. Before long the behaviour can become obsessive and compulsive, and the disorder takes over the 'reward centre' in the cat's brain (see page 160). The more the cat licks and

RIGHT **Cats, especially the long-haired breeds, will groom themselves frequently in order to enhance their hunter's ability.**

grooms, the better it feels temporarily – but the disorder can quickly make the cat exceed normal grooming behaviour and it becomes locked into a neurotic 'stress-calm-stress' cycle. A cat that is over-grooming to such an extent as to create bald patches should be referred to an animal behaviourist for treatment.

Why is over-grooming behaviour occurring?

Over-grooming in cats occurs because of the effects of stress and the self-rewarding chemical mechanism on the brain. The area in the cat's brain that registers and deals with chemical reward (serotonin and dopamine) also deals with addiction, fixation and obsession. Once the repetitive behaviour of grooming, or more specifically licking itself over and over again in the form of stereotypical behaviour, begins to over-stimulate the reward centre in the brain, the cat finds itself locked into an addiction that can be extremely damaging to its physical well-being.

How should I best deal with over-grooming behaviour?

It is easy to reinforce this behaviour by becoming concerned and inadvertently communicating your anxiety to the cat. Once attention is given, the cat may stop the behaviour but then over-dependency and more stress can be promoted. It is possible to use training discs (see page 164) to signal 'non-reward' when the

behaviour occurs, instead of reinforcing it with concerned attention. Establishing the cause of the stress and thus being able to deal with the known triggers for problem behaviour may require professional advice.

Why does my cat suddenly decide to attack me when I am stroking it?

Contented cats can be stroked until human attention spans are tested to the limit. However, cats that want to control the cat-owner relationship will break off contact when they deem it to be over. To emphasize control, a nervous or aggressive cat will display its potential dominance over an owner by abruptly ending the interactive session.

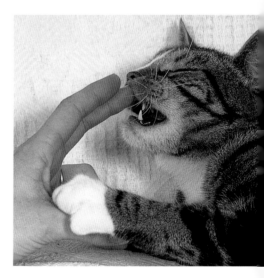

ABOVE Cats who want to be in charge of the relationship may use an aggressive act to control owner-interaction.

Why does my cat suddenly bring out its claws and scratch my hand?

Cats do not 'stroke' each other. Human stroking of a cat may be perceived in the feline mind as 'marking' behaviour, with the human transferring their body scent onto the cat during tactile contact. The dominant cat will consider this marking behaviour on the part of the owner to be a violation of its body space and will use aggression to make its point. Once a cat learns that its owner will react by withdrawing their hand, it knows that its aggression will create the desired response every time.

Why does my cat suddenly chase around the house in what appears to be a 'mad fit'?

Most cat owners are bemused when they first encounter this behaviour. The cat will suddenly appear to 'fly' down stairs without touching the treads. If there are other cats in the home, a frenzied feline will often be following in hot pursuit. Vases can fall, phantom shadows are chased and attacked, a settee will be vaulted and curtains climbed. There can also be rough and tumble and vocalization during this bout of apparent feline madness, and there may be numerous stops and starts. The common pattern is that the behaviour occurs on a daily basis.

This syndrome appears to affect most cats, although house cats are thought to experience it most often. Cats that are content to stay indoors rarely expend the same amount of energy as even relatively lazy outdoor cats, yet they often eat the same amount. These periods of intense physical effort are about a cat expending energy in one concentrated burst. A cat's personality can also play a big part in how often this behaviour occurs.

Although the owner rarely becomes actively involved, when the cat suddenly stares at them with a 'look at me' face it is asking the human to play along with its apparently psychotic game. This form of intense and energetic cat behaviour is displaced stalking, hunting and play behaviour. All play behaviour is basic training for becoming a successful predator. The cat is looking for interaction from another cat, which in the cat's perception can be the owner, and instinct takes over during an adrenalin-driven game. The owner simply becomes part of this stalking and hunting game.

There are many forms of feline play behaviour that can be seen as adaptations. For example:
- Cats crash through newspapers or paper bags so enthusiastically because bursting through materials is not much different to bursting through undergrowth or leaves.
- Cats wiggle their back legs as they get ready to pounce on a bit of fluff on the carpet because this prepares them for a leap – a kind of balance check before they pounce on their prey.

This type of play in domestic situations involves modes of behaviour that are linked to prey stalking, attacking and predation in nature.

ABOVE **Cats naturally compete with each other because they are solitary predators and this is their instinctive behaviour.**

Why do my cats fight each other?

Cats are solitary predators. Domesticated cats can adapt to extended socialization, but those that are content to do so will usually have been kept together as kittens. There are situations when artificial feral groups come together due to a scarcity of food or lack of ownership. Kittens brought up together may show mutual socialization and are usually less aggressive towards each other in domestication. However, all wild kittens will develop competitive behaviour towards each other.

Cats will fight over territory, access to food or the attention of owners and, if entire, potential sexual partners. In nature, the loser skulks away to fight over another territory that is not so well defended, or to fight the same battle another day. In the home, the competitive battle lines can be redrawn and refought on a daily basis.

How can I stop my cat bullying another cat?

It is possible to reduce competition and therefore aggression between cats by examining the aspects where the disputes arise. Research indicates that the main causes of continuing disputes between house cats is over access to owners and to areas in the inner home territory. When one cat is stroked or fussed by the owner, the other may feel its ownership of the human is being questioned. 'Owner scents' can be detected on the cat even if the activity has not been observed by the bullying cat. The cause of an act of aggression may have its roots in an action between the owner and the cat that occurred in the hours preceding the violence.

An owner who has competing cats in the same home should reduce petting and fussing, and offer enhanced security for the cats by installing extra bolt holes (boxes, igloos), plus more litter trays and scratching posts, to help combat territorial and ownership disputes.

It can be extremely disturbing for owners to see pets fight and aggression is stressful for both the bully and the bullied. By becoming more detached from your cats you can help to reduce competition between them, but it does mean a reduction in the contact that is the main purpose of owning companion cats.

Why does my cat chase off other cats that come into our garden?

Your cat does this for exactly the same reason that you would chase off uninvited human trespassers in and around your home. A house cat views its home and surrounding property as its own territory. As far as a cat is concerned, its territory must be defended, although this is dependent on personality and some are more determined in this behaviour than others.

How can I punish my cat for bad behaviour?

The term 'bad behaviour' used in relation to cats is extremely subjective. Almost all the common forms of feline antisocial behaviour would be perfectly normal in nature:
- Scratching furniture is not too far removed from scratching trees.
- Spraying on objects is no different in the home to outside it.
- Displaying aggression towards a competitor who is attempting to invade the cat's home territory, steal food and demand attention from an owner is perfectly reasonable behaviour from its perspective.

Nonetheless, there are occasions when we do want to inform an otherwise perfect cat that scratching the new furniture will not endear them to the family and should not be tried. Aversion methods – such as spraying water at the cat – to punish or stop problem behaviour can not only increase anxious behaviour but also lead to mistrust between cat and owner and so are rarely effective. Shouting and hitting should never be directed towards a cat, for the same reasons.

In behavioural therapy, it is recommended that a sound-signal should be used that has first been associated with the removal of a food treat. Training discs are a sound-signal training aid that have been used successfully in this way. They make a distinctive sound and, once conditioned into a cat's subconscious, can be used to stop unwanted behaviour (see page 164).

What are training discs?

Training discs are used to signal 'non-reward' and 'end-behaviour'. They can be used successfully to replace ineffective punishment strategies such as shouting at your cat.

Training discs are tambourine-like brass discs threaded on a short cord. Their sound first becomes associated with non-reward by setting up a special association session. Wait for your cat to show an unwanted behaviour (such as scratching furniture), show it a food treat, lightly sound the discs and then walk away with the treat and discs. After a number of repetitions, the cat will associate the sound of the discs with removal of a food treat.

After a period of use, the training discs will automatically signal a 'non-reward' to the cat, and by association this will discourage the cat from displaying the unwanted behaviour. This strategy also removes the need for the owner to appear to pay attention to the cat in order to deal with the situation, which can actually reinforce the behaviour.

Why does my cat scratch the furniture?

Scratching behaviour is common to all felines, large and small. In nature, it is a fundamental part of marking behaviour, usually directed towards tree trunks, to denote territorial possession. In the absence of trees inside most owners' living areas, the cat seeks out alternatives – wallpaper and the furniture is often all

that is available. The cat is merely following its natural instincts and is not being actively destructive.

How do I stop my cat from scratching furniture?

The inclusion of several purpose-made scratching posts in the home is essential for a happy and contented cat. These are available to buy from pet stores. For details of how to encourage your cat to use the scratching posts, see opposite.

Why does my cat scratch at one particular place on the carpet?

Cats return to the same places to mark, either by scratching or through scent-marking (or even a combination of both). This is because they deem it to be a location within the territory that they need to show is already possessed. Once a spot has been marked, the cat will pick up the scent-tag every time it returns and the need to re-mark becomes foremost and then habitual.

How should I deal with my cat when he damages carpets and furniture?

If the behaviour occurs while you are present, you can use training discs (see left) to interrupt the cat before the damage is done. There are often clear signs that a cat is about to mark an object. It may sniff the target and then start to rub up against it, with its tail fully raised. If you sound the training discs at this point, the behaviour can be interrupted before the cat moves on into the next, destructive stage of scratching (or spraying).

Will double-sided adhesive tape applied to furniture stop a cat scratching it?

Some experts suggest that double-sided carpet tape applied to furniture or in a particular spot will stop a cat from scratching there. However, in some cases it may simply deter the cat from scratching in one place and redirect it to another area or object.

How can I stop destructive behaviour?

Cats need to scratch, especially vertical objects, in order to mark their perceived territory and to make it safe. The best method of dealing with this when destructive scratching becomes problem behaviour is to harness the need and redirect it to a more appropriate place.

Offering a cat several tall indoor scratching posts is often a successful strategy. Most scratching posts available in pet stores are at least 1 m (3ft 3in) in height. Research suggests that a cat needs to stretch out fully when scratching a vertical surface, in order to be fully satisfied that it has left its territorial mark.

ABOVE **Cats need to explore and make their mark on vertical surfaces to establish their territory. Try and encourage them to use scratching posts instead.**

How can I get my cat to scratch his post instead of the furniture?

You can encourage a cat's interest in a scratching post by using catnip and food treats. Catnip is a plant extract (see page 178) that is available from pet stores as a spray or dried leaves. Place food treats at the base of the post to attract the cat to it initially, then use the clicker system of signalling and rewarding good behaviour (see below). Sound the clicker and give a food reward when the cat uses the post. Eventually, through the effects of classical conditioning (see page 145), you will be able to click several times for the cat using the scratching post (each click is a reward), to enhance this behaviour by stimulating serotonin (a feel-good hormone) at the 'reward centre' in the cat's brain (see page 160).

What is a clicker?

A clicker is a thumb-sized plastic unit enclosing a tin flap that makes a distinctive 'click-click' sound when you depress it. Once associated with a tasty morsel of food over several sessions in a week, the double click can then be used to signal every time a food treat is about to be given.

Eventually, in a true Pavlovian response (classical conditioning, see page 145), the click sound will become the reward, and every positive act (a stroke, verbal congratulations in a happy tone of voice or a food treat) that is associated with it becomes a reinforcer or promoter of whatever behaviour you want the cat to perform. The 'conditioned' click sound is thus associated with food or treats, which will encourage a natural response from the cat due to its innate desire to eat.

Once it has become established as a reward for the cat, the clicker sound signal can be used to promote good behaviour, but it should always be associated with a food treat as well as verbal praise or a stroke.

How do I introduce my new cat to my dog?

Your approach should be geared to the known attitude of the dog towards cats.

- If the dog is friendly towards cats, play a 'click and treat' retrieval game with the dog on a lead while the cat is exploring the same room. Distract the dog if it gets boisterous towards the cat.
- If the dog is known to show aggression or hyperactivity towards cats, it should be muzzled as a precaution.
- If the non-aggressive dog becomes boisterous towards the cat, use a reward (toy or food) to entice it away.

BELOW Stroking may not necessarily help to socialize a cat to new people but offering food treats can help.

- If the dog displays aggression, lead-walk it away from the cat and then separate them for the time being until a socialization programme can be undertaken, in which the introduction is made more gradually until the dog becomes desensitized to the presence of the cat.
- If your dog is aggressive towards the new cat, it is important to be calm and not to make the situation more 'exciting' by your concern or dramatic attention. This behaviour on your part can make the introduction and then reinforce its connection with hyperactivity or aggression on the dog's part, thereby promoting its antisocial behaviour.

Why does my cat hide when my partner first arrives?

Some cats become entirely dependent on their owner. As 'replacement litter mothers' or 'replacement lead cats', humans can easily turn the relationship into one that encourages feline over-dependency and nervousness. In this situation, when a partner first appears they are probably viewed by the cat as an extremely large competitor.

An 'intelligent' cat, in feline terms, knows it is best to run and hide and be able to 'fight another day' than to be caught up in a potential battle that cannot be won. Eventually, a cat must make the logical decision that the partner is not an aggressive competitor for 'resources' within the home, and usually relaxes the nervous behaviours it was showing.

How can I encourage my cat to like my new partner?

There is nothing like 'cupboard love' to modify a cat's problem behaviour towards a new partner. Nevertheless, it is not advisable for a new partner to attempt any physical interaction, such as stroking or picking up the cat. This could be seen as both threatening and an invasion of the cat's body space. In addition, there could also be a perceived competitive aspect between the combinations male cat/male partner and female cat/female partner.

Clicker training (see opposite) prior to introduction can help in this situation. The partner should initially ignore the cat, then gradually, over a few days, begin to be involved in introducing the clicker method of rewarding an appearance by the cat. At this time, the known partner would introduce the food treats in response to the new partner signalling with the clicker.

How can I encourage my cat to mix with my partner's cats?

Introducing adult cats to each other is probably one of the most difficult tasks involving feline behaviour. It is almost equivalent to human adults coming together in a second marriage, each introducing grown children to the situation. Expecting the children to be best friends straight away may be somewhat naive, but this could happen after explanations and discussions. However, it is obviously impossible to discuss any arrangements, house moves and other changes with cats! Nor will they understand human-initiated events as they unfold.

In the best-case scenario, the cats are all fairly secure and content, and will treat each other as non-threatening. In this situation, a feline stand-off will usually occur until they accept that the new social situation is long term.

In the worst-case scenario, the feline equivalent of a world war will break out that may involve aggression, toilet problems and spraying. The poor loser will want to leave home or will hide away in the nearest bolt hole, developing acute withdrawn behaviour as a sign of stress. This situation can be just as stressful for owners.

There are several steps you can take:

- To start the socialization process, use cat carriers – or, better still, crates as they offer more space – to separate the cats physically but keep them close by.
- If cats can be fed together, this is an important step forward.
- It is vital that owners remain relaxed as 'observers' around the cats, because any apprehension or fear will be quickly transmitted to them through body language and pheromones that may be linked to nervousness.
- It is also advisable not to attempt to fuss, cuddle, talk to or encourage a cat to sit close by you in this situation. When you stroke the cats you are effectively 'marking' them by transferring scents, and this can also fuel competition between the cats.
- If and when they are outside the crates, the cats should be offered a number of safe havens or 'dens' in the form of strong cardboard boxes scattered about the rooms, so that the bullied cat can have a place into which to retreat that offers some protection and security.

How can I get my cats to accept my partner's dog?

There are a number of steps to take when introducing your cats to the dog.

1 Ideally, the dog should first be contained in a covered crate or indoor kennel in the room where the 'controlled introduction' will be made. The cats should not be in the room when the dog is first placed in the crate.

2 Place a number of different treats on saucers or in small containers around the room. Introduce one or more new scratching posts, pre-sprayed with catnip (see page 178).

3 Allow the cats to enter and explore the room in their own time. If they use the scratching post(s) and take food, this is significant progress. You can give the dog some food treats as a reward for being in the crate.

4 Following this initial period (15–30 minutes) of exposure, and assuming there have been positive signs rather than aggression (some cats will investigate the sides and top of the crate, and this may encourage the dog to react by smelling or trying to lick them), lead the dog from the crate, out of the room and into another part of the home. Again, reward the dog for displaying any composure.

5 If all went well during the first period of exposure, return with the dog after 15 minutes and repeat the process.

6 If there was much spitting and snarling, offer the cats an extended period (1–2 hours) in the introduction room in which to calm down. Do not offer the cats or the dog excessive attention or eye contact, in order to reduce owner triggers for problem behaviours. If the dog is showing no sign of accepting the cats during a number of controlled introductions, you will need the help of a professional behaviourist.

7 If the initial exposure has been free of any disturbed behaviour by either the cats or the dog, move on to the next stage. Click and treat the dog while 'controlled' contact is undertaken, with the dog outside the crate and the cats allowed to wander around the room. Never force the dog to approach the cats or vice versa, as this will create a negative association for both.

How can I best help my cat that is frightened of loud noises?

Nervous cats can sometimes become hyper-alert and this makes them acutely sensitive to any loud or unusual noises. Once frightened by a particular sound, a cat will normally be triggered into the fight, freeze or flight mode of behaviour that is used in nature to aid survival. Once a cat decides to make a run for it, adrenalin helps to boost its physical capabilities. In this situation most cats will seek out the nearest available bolt hole – in the home, this can be a cupboard, behind kitchen work units, under the bed or inside the narrowest of crevices. Outdoors, the bolt hole might be under a shed, up a tree or behind any available obstacle.

Do not make too much fuss of your cat in this situation, because any concern could be interpreted as a mutual fear of the sound. It is important to provide a nervous cat with a ready-made bolt hole such as an igloo-type cat bed, which can be lined with an old item of your clothing. If this is worn temporarily it will have been scented, and its presence in the artificial bolt hole can act as a security blanket for the cat.

Why does my cat spray in the house?

Although spraying is usually associated with entire tom cats, it is not exclusive to them. Both neutered and un-neutered cats display this behaviour when competition occurs for a known territory or resource and feline ownership is being challenged. As spraying is part of natural territorial behaviour in cats, the need to perform urine marking increases when there are reasons for a cat to be insecure in the home and surrounding property.

Nervous cats are most likely to spray or urinate in the home, and the onset of this behaviour can be linked to stress, including house moves, changes in the home and family, the introduction of other cats, and competition or aggression between cats.

How can I stop my cat from spraying in the house?

It is advisable not to react adversely when a cat has sprayed because that will just make matters worse. One of the best methods for dealing with a spraying cat is to redirect the cat's need to mark the home territory in a different way or to a more appropriate place.

Tall scratching posts (see page 165) are extremely valuable in this situation, because when a cat 'scratch marks' it is making its territory secure in the same way as during urine marking. By using the clicker system (see page 166) to reinforce the use of the scratching post, the cat's need to urine mark can be significantly reduced.

Why does my cat defecate and urinate in the home?

Cats use faeces and urine to mark territory. In some instances, such as when there are disputes over the use of a litter tray or aggressive competition from cats in the neighbourhood, a home cat will defecate elsewhere. Sometimes faeces are placed on a bed, in the middle of a carpet or even close to the litter tray, but in the case of territorial disputes that include the litter tray, not perfectly in the tray. This behaviour is closely linked to feline and territorial insecurity.

How can I stop my cat defecating and urinating in the house?

Never scold a cat for this behaviour or it will simply get worse. The first thing to do is offer the cat extra litter trays in different locations throughout the house. If faeces and/or urine are discovered in the house, make sure your cat does not watch the next step – wait until it is outside or in another part of the house. Transfer the faeces into a new litter tray and place this tray close to the place where the problem is occurring. Mop up the urine with absorbent kitchen paper and place this in the litter tray. This method can deceive a cat into believing it has used the tray, and will encourage it to over-mark in the tray with urine and faeces on its next visits.

Why does my cat toilet inappropriately indoors in the same places?

Cats like to over-mark where they have already urinated or defecated. This procedure fulfils their continual need to make their perceived territory secure. No matter what cleaning method has been used, when a cat can smell its own scent it will usually return to the same spot and re-mark. In some cases this is a daily occurrence and until the problem is dealt with correctly it will happen over again.

If you install a scratching post in the most common place for marking, you can then encourage the cat to redirect its behaviour to scratching rather than using body wastes for marking (see left).

Why does my cat spray on plugs and sockets?

Cats tend to over-mark objects that have already been marked – even if these items have been human-marked. Because we tend to handle electrical points and appliance plugs on a frequent basis, this makes our scent strong on them and thus makes them attractive to marking-obsessed cats.

Why does my cat leave faeces just outside the litter tray?

There are some common myths surrounding this irritating phenomenon. One is that these mishaps occur because the litter tray needs cleaning; another that the tray is too small and should be larger or covered to prevent this problem from recurring.

Closer to the truth is that this behaviour – which is closely linked to feline middening (see right) – often occurs in households that have more than one cat and this can lead to disputes over the use of the litter tray. Another factor with adopted cats is that they may have experienced competitive behaviour related to the use of litter trays in the past.

A good plan to try to cure this problem is to transfer the faeces into the litter tray when the cat is not watching, in order to deceive it into believing it had placed the results of its toilet in the tray (see above left). This is the feline version of moving the newspaper when toilet-training a puppy.

What is 'middening'?

Cats – whether domesticated, feral or wild – usually dig into soft earth or leaf litter and bury faeces. The success of the litter trays used by house cats in the home is based on this principle. However, faeces are also utilized by cats in a behaviour that is known as 'middening'. This is where faeces are deliberately placed at the periphery of an established or disputed territory and is intended to show potential ownership, much in the same way as when a cat sprays. A number of animals are known to display middening behaviour, including some canines such as foxes and wolves.

In domesticated cats that are displaying middening behaviour, the faeces are often openly placed in hall or lounge walkways, close to a litter tray, sometimes barely inside the home close to where a cat flap is positioned, or on beds. This behaviour has been noted to occur in cats that are in dispute with other cats or by nervous cats suffering from feline insecurity,

Why does my cat spray on the toaster?

This behaviour is not easily explained. It may simply be that most toasters are used on a daily basis and are therefore handled by owners who leave their scent behind. As the toaster warms up to heat the bread the human scent may be amplified. This might make the toaster more attractive as an object for over-marking behaviour.

Will neutering my cat stop indoor 'toilet problems'?

Unfortunately, neutering a cat will not have any effect on the causes of indoor spraying and problem toilet behaviour. Almost all the cats under treatment with behaviourists are house pets and they are usually neutered at around 6 months. This is done at this age to prevent the developing toms and queens from performing spraying or urine- and faeces-marking behaviours, and the behaviours becoming habitualized.

The main advantage to neutering (and the reason to have it done) is to stop cats breeding through accidental matings; preventing habitualization of spraying is a secondary advantage. However, just because a cat has been neutered this does not mean that it will not develop the insecurities that can perhaps lead to indoor toileting.

Should I shout at my cat for 'messing' in the house?

Any dramatic response by you will simply increase the feline nervousness that is often the root cause of the behaviour. It is important to be calm and to offer extra litter trays and opportunities for the cat to 'mark' in other ways, such as with the introduction of tall scratching posts (see page 165).

How should I clean up the 'mess' my cat has made?

It is important that you clean up urine and faeces only when the cat cannot see what you are doing. If the mess is cleaned up in front of the cat, it may see this behaviour as your over-marking its marking. In these instances, the cat is driven to over-mark the cleaned area, although this will often take place under cover of darkness or when you are out of the house.

What disinfectant should I use to clean up my cat's 'mess'?

Many strong-smelling disinfectants, in particular those including ammonia, can attract a cat to perform over-marking behaviour. It is best to use a biological cleaning spray, available from most supermarkets or pet stores, that utilizes enzymes to break down the body scents used by cats to mark, so neutralizing rather than over-marking it.

How can I stop my cat's toileting problems?

You need to examine possible causes that are driving the cat to behave 'inappropriately' in terms of human expectations. Usually, feline disputes, feline nervousness or over-dependency on you, the cat's owner, are involved, especially if the behaviour occurs with a cat that has not previously displayed any toileting problems. A newly introduced cat, particularly one that has been rescued and adopted, may be responding to competition from an existing cat, or to changes and disturbances in its territory and breaks in previous attachments to other humans.

Installing extra litter trays and scratching posts can have a positive effect on a nervous cat, as can restricting the home territory to a single room until the cat feels secure and the behaviour has subsided. In some cases, you may need to obtain professional advice from an animal behaviourist following referral from your veterinary surgeon.

Is it possible to use a cat's natural smell to stop it spraying?

There is a simple, practical technique that involves extracting a cat's natural body scent and transferring it to a target that has been repeatedly marked. Rub a clean, damp cloth (or unscented wipe) gently down the flanks of the cat so that the cloth begins to absorb the cat's body scent. Then rub the cloth on the object that the cat is spraying – the theory behind this technique is that the cat will resist marking it in the belief that it has already done so.

The evidence suggests that this can be effective in cases where marking behaviour is mild. However, this method has proved to be ineffective in those cases where the marking behaviour is acute, when the cat is suffering from feline insecurity and the problem behaviour has become habitualized.

Why does my cat demand attention all the time? Is this a good thing?

Owners who truly 'love' their cats are often pleased when their cat continually wants to interact with them. Sometimes the human ego is over-stimulated by companion animals displaying such interest and dependency. However, in many instances such close interaction with a cat that is always attention-seeking leads to the development of feline over-dependency. In addition, there are also cases where the owners cannot take time away from the cats for events ranging from holidays to hospitalization.

Cats that are intensely involved with their owners will often develop problem behaviours linked to hyper-attachment, especially if the owner has to take time away from home. In these instances, the over-dependent cat becomes extremely stressed and, in acute cases, can begin to develop a separation-related disorder (see page 187), spray around the home and display acute withdrawn behaviours.

It is advisable to encourage independent, confident behaviour in your cat, as this will lead to a more even relationship and ensures feline and human contentment in the long term.

Why does my cat want to sleep in our bedroom but is then active during the night?

A cat that enjoys a close relationship with its owner wants to be involved in all activities that occur within the inner

territory (home). The reason cats love to be in the bedroom is that humans spend almost half their time at home in this special 'inner sanctum'. This is the place where we leave the strongest scent trail (see right) and, from the cat's perspective, perform marking behaviour.

The conflict comes with the fact that although we spend a great deal of time in the bedroom, we are generally asleep and inactive during this period. Cats, being the closest nocturnal animals we keep as companion pets, probably find this paradox extremely confusing. It is difficult for them to understand that their owners do not necessarily follow the same daily active/inactive patterns as they do!

Is it advisable for our cat to be allowed into our bedroom?

The short answer is 'no'. The main reason why you should not allow your cat into the bedroom is because, apart from some rare exceptions, they are at their most active at night (see page 181). Only real night-owls would wish to be kept awake throughout the night by a cat that wants to play, go out, come back in and so on.

There are also many secondary reasons why you may want to consider whether or not your cat should be allowed into your bedroom:

• A nervous or distressed cat may mark

OPPOSITE **Cats are best kept away from bedrooms because of the potential for marking where humans leave powerful scents.**

the bedding with urine and faeces, and through spraying.
• A cat may begin grooming while you are asleep, which can lead to more loose hairs being spread around and subsequently breathed in. This can result in allergic reactions and poor sleeping patterns.
• Some owners sweat profusely during the night (which is one of the reasons there is so much human scent in bedding) and a cat sleeping close to an owner can become over-warm and then active.

How can I stop my cat scratching at any door that is closed?

The main problem door for attention-seeking cats is the bedroom door. Often the owner finds it easier to allow the cat access to the bedroom rather than have it continually scratching to enter.

One successful method of dealing with this problem is to place a large scratching post outside the bedroom, at the point between the door and the door frame. This has to be drawn into place as the door is closed. The cat will tend to scratch the post a few times, feel that its frustration has been relieved, and then wander off to perform different night-time activities.

Why is my cat bored with her toys? How do I make toys interesting?

Kittens will play with any object that attracts their curiosity, from a ball of wool

to clothes buttons. Cats do not select the toys that their owner buys. Most cat toys are designed (and deliberately humanized) in order to attract the owner to buy them. For example, many mouse-shaped toys remain static on the floor where the owner first places them, while the cat stands by with confusion written on its face – this is not how a real mouse should behave.

The reality is that very few cat toys are interactive without the owner animating them. Some cat toys are made to contain (or can be sprayed with) catnip (see page 178) – this scent can often be the stimulus for an active cat to treat the toy as interesting and even as a 'mouse'. Otherwise, you can draw toys along the floor on string and dangle them to tantalize your cat.

ABOVE **House cats will play with toys but they also look for and enjoy interaction through them with their owners.**

What are the best games to play with my cat?

Active adult cats and growing kittens thrive on the movement of items of all kinds. This will stimulate their instinctive predatory reactions to pounce, snatch and bite.

'Track toys' are excellent for encouraging play. These often come in the form of dinnerplate-size circular units that have an outer groove along which a table-tennis-size ball can run. Cats can bat the ball around and around until they temporarily tire and

walk away. Some track toys also have scratch centres and a vertical spring with a bobble toy on top. This type of 'interaction' toy will encourage a cat to play independently from you.

It is also possible to announce social play sessions by offering titbits or toys pulled along by a string. Young kittens and some older cats love interactive games that encourage normal prowl, chase and catch behaviours. A 'fishing rod' with an elastic line and some kind of feathered toy attached can also be extremely successful.

A recently introduced cat-only interactive toy involves an automatic unit that sends a mouse flying around beyond the circumference of the base area for the cat to catch. This toy can be set on a timer to start and stop as required in order to keep it interesting. It is also useful if the cat is on its own in the house.

ABOVE Cats are often stimulated by movement and enjoy watching the changing shapes and colours on television.

Can I create my own cat toys?

One cat owner created a simple but highly successful game that required no effort on her part. This consisted simply of introducing table-tennis balls into a shower tray that sloped centrally into a drain. The indoor cat played with this for several 20-minute periods through the day, batting the balls around the shower unit. The owner used this to keep the cat happy while she was at work, introducing the balls just before she left the house. The balls could also be indelibly marked with patterns to make them even more interesting.

Can cats watch television and understand the images?

Cats are attracted by movement rather than by colour. There are many stories from cat owners of their pets attempting to catch bowls, tennis balls or pool or snooker balls when these games are shown on television. A cat attracted to the movement will often leap up at the screen and attempt to catch the ball. The same cat will sit and stare patiently at an aquarium or goldfish bowl and periodically make a leap and pouncing snatch at the fish.

How can I stop a dog from chasing my cat?

Certain dog breeds (particularly working dogs like collies and terriers) seem to enjoy chasing cats. This is akin to a young child chasing pigeons. The cat racing away stimulates instinctive predator-prey responses in the dog; in children, it is usually to see the flight reaction of the birds.

Cat-chasing in dogs can be reduced with the use of a remote-controlled scent collar that is based on aversion principles. The collar works up to 200 m (220 yd) away when used with a long antenna. When you press a button on the unit, this triggers a short or long burst of a powerful citronella scent or an odourless jet from a reservoir on the dog's collar.

How can I get my cat to use the litter tray? He seems to be slow on the uptake.

Cats that are slow to use a litter tray can be encouraged through reward. The clicker system (see page 166) is extremely successful if there is occasional use of the litter tray. If the cat refuses to use the tray at all, then one method that has proved successful is to transfer urine or faeces that the cat has left elsewhere into the litter tray, to deceive the cat into believing that it has already used the tray. This principle is based on the fact that cats are keen to over-mark where they have previously marked (see pages 172–173).

ABOVE Cats will use litter trays providing they are covered or placed in a quiet area in the home. A covered tray helps prevents spills.

Why do cats like catnip?

The catnip plant (Nepeta cataria), sometimes called catmint, produces a distinctive smell through the oil in its leaves (nepetalactone). This oil scent is well known for sending cats into a relaxed state of euphoria.

Can I grow my own catnip plant?

You can grow catnip (*Nepeta cataria*) in the garden or even in a window box. This plant is fairly easy to grow although many owners find it easier to buy bags of dried leaves or catnip sprays.

Can I teach my cat to be careful when crossing roads?

It is extremely difficult to train a cat to stop and look before crossing a busy road. It might be possible to clicker train a young cat by maintaining its attention at a roadside and only sounding the clicker and treating when it is safe to cross. Like all animals, cats have an instinctive drive to survive and quickly learn what and where is dangerous. The wary cat will wait before crossing a road, and fortunately most roads are quieter late a night (when cats are active) than during rush hours and daylight times.

A busy road is most dangerous when a cat is being pursued and all sense of fear is directed towards escape rather than the traffic. It is when a cat is distracted that most road accidents occur.

Is it all right to allow another cat into my home?

The short answer is 'no'. Allowing another cat into the inner territory of the home is the equivalent (to your cat) of allowing a burglar into your home and openly inviting him to use your food and take your possessions. There may be exceptions where two cats are actually socialized with each other, but these would be rare.

Why is my cat hesitant about going outside?

A cat that refuses to go outdoors into a known territory is often the subject of feline bullying. This is very similar to the reaction of a bullied child who wants to avoid going to school. It is the fear of what the outside world (or school, in the case of the child) represents that is creating the reluctance, rather than a judgement on the world as a place to live in. Often the bullying cat has taken over part of the territory that your cat feels belongs to him. And this cat will defend its 'new' territory fiercely.

How can I stop another cat from trying to bully my cat?

This is impossible without shadowing your cat constantly to protect it on every single one of its excursions into the outer territory. In outdoor situations, most aggressive cats will not force their dominance onto another to such an extent that physical injuries will result. Usually the subdominant cat will either back off or take flight and retreat to a bolt hole.

Sadly, some cats react very badly to the continual presence of a bully cat and will often retreat into the home, perhaps even permanently.

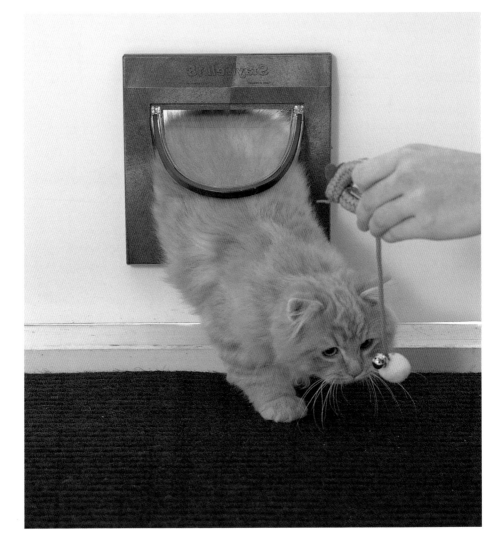

How do I get my cat to use the cat flap?

The best method is through reward.
You will need two people for this. One remains indoors with the cat while the other is on the other side of the cat flap offering a tantalizing food treat or toy. Few cats, apart from the acutely neurotic, will refuse to pass through the flap to

take a fresh prawn, mincemeat or small piece of ham or for a game with their favourite toy. Once through, the method can be reversed to encourage the cat to return through the flap.

Why does my cat constantly cry at the bedroom door at night?

The hours when you are asleep may be the only time that a cat with a strong dependency is separated from its owner. Its behaviour then reflects the frustration and stress that separation creates.

Night-time activity is very high on a cat's personal agenda and being frustrated at this time will cause an emotional cat to cry. If the owner gives into the demands of such an attention-seeking cat, it will then want to stay in the bedroom every night and will also express a desire to interact during the hours of darkness.

Why does my cat lick my face and try to wake me up at night?

Cats are essentially nocturnal animals that are naturally more active at night. Humans, on the other hand, need to sleep when cats are at their most lively. A cat licking its owner's face is not only obtaining scent information but is also performing allogrooming (mutual grooming) behaviour (see page 144). More often than not, the owner wakes up and the cat's behaviour has been successful. (The next step, as far as the cat is concerned would be for the owner to leave the house via the cat flap and perform a spot of territorial behaviour, some marking and prey hunting. Few owners, however, are so committed to their cats that they feel the urge to proceed to this next step.)

ABOVE **Cats who are particularly dependent on their owner and find separation stressful may resort to crying outside their bedroom door at night.**

Why does my cat go to the toilet on my bed and not in the litter tray?

Cats' toileting is not just about urinating and defecating. They have evolved to use body wastes to leave behind marking information or feline scent signals that are messages for each other. In nature, these scent messages are intended to offer information to other cats about territorial boundaries, sex, oestrus cycle, and gender-linked testosterone and oestrogen levels. The scent information possibly offers other details as well, although experts debate how much information forms the 'full scent picture'.

The onset of feline sexual maturity can lead to some behavioural problems in domesticated cats due to instinctive drives. However, a neutered cat can also display these marking behaviours because, while its sex drive is significantly reduced, the cat retains its gender since this aspect of sexuality is governed by the brain. Neutered cats that are nervous are therefore just as likely as entire cats to perform inappropriate marking behaviour.

Human scent on a bed is as strong as or stronger than anywhere else in the home (see pages 175), and a nervous cat or one that is embroiled in a dispute with another cat will over-mark where the human has marked. This could be an alliance behaviour towards the owner or possibly competitive marking behaviour against the owner because the cat cannot win against the other cat. But it is most certainly not disobedient behaviour just for the sake of it.

Why else might my cat urinate in the wrong place?

When a cat defecates indoors away from the usual place (litter tray or garden), it is attempting to make the perceived inner territory more secure. However, marking behaviour will also provide the cat with temporary relief from any emotional problem behaviours such as aggression, competition or nervousness, through the 'reward hormone' serotonin (see page 160). The surge in serotonin is, however, just a temporary 'fix', as this hormone is quickly reabsorbed.

Why has my cat defecated and urinated on a guest bed?

The presence of a stranger in the home can disturb a nervous cat. This is because the cat likes its world to be as consistent and unthreatening as possible. The visiting family member or friend may be viewed as a threat or a competitor for resources such as food, territory and possessive contact with the owner. The simplest way to establish feline possession is to mark the object, or over-mark where another cat has marked – hence the bed becoming the target.

Why does my cat follow me on walks? I am worried about him getting lost.

This problem can be fairly common with cats that have friendly, out-going personalities. However, it is not the case with those that have an over-dependent relationship with their owners. A cat with a bubbly personality wants to explore the surrounding territory with his favourite 'human-cat' and, taking the owner's lead in these matters, will follow until an event interrupts the togetherness.

Most cats have a basic 'memory map' of the area surrounding their home and will add extra parts to the map as they explore further. The danger comes when a walk takes in busy roads and junctions or involves the owner climbing into a taxi or bus. These situations could leave the cat a long way from home and slightly disorientated.

If there is any concern about your cat's following behaviour, use a specially chosen walk to:

- Introduce some longer-than-normal stops. These extended stationary periods will eventually lead to boredom on the cat's part and he will set off for home.
- Alternatively, get a family member to use food treats to encourage the cat to return home with them.

Do cats need exercise?

All animals benefit from being fit. In addition, physical health is linked to psychological well-being, so a fit cat is probably a happy one too.

A contented house cat that does little besides lounging around and eating will soon become overweight and slothful, which is no better for cats than people.

You will need to motivate such a cat to venture out and about, at least when the weather is good. Some exercise can be encouraged indoors by making string lures with a delicious food treat attached, which can be dangled tantalizingly over the banisters or dragged along the floor to induce the cat to chase them and so get some exercise.

How should I introduce my cat to a new cat?

It is not possible to introduce cats formally to each other in the same way sociable humans make introductions. To an established cat, an additional cat is an intruder, a 'cat burglar' who is looking to steal important resources including warmth, food, inner and outer territory, and contact with the lead cat (the human owner).

There are a number of important contributing factors to take into account when introducing cats to each other:

- If the established cat is happy and contented, it could be that its personality will not create too many problems when it comes into contact with a young, non-threatening kitten. However, even contented adult cats rarely form an immediate social balance with each other – there is usually some form of hierarchy.
- If the established cat is highly dependent on its owner, then there is a strong likelihood that feline war will break out.

Once you have decided to bring a newcomer into the home, then physical control factors become important if aggression is to be avoided. The

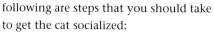
following are steps that you should take to get the cat socialized:

1 Place the new cat in a closed 'introduction' room alone to wander around freely and explore for 10–15 minutes. The introduction room should contain at least one tall scratching post and two litter trays, preferably covered. You, the owner, should take the role of calm observer and be sitting down. It is important throughout not to stroke the cats, and to ignore any hissing or spitting.

2 Leave the room and return with the established cat in a travel crate or cat carrier. Place it in the introduction room (if it is an open-wire crate, cover with a cloth to offer 'territorial security') and close the door. The crate offers security and protection for both the aggressive and the subdominant cat. Ideally, the crate should not be one that has been used for veterinary visits, as this may have a negative association. Allow 30 minutes for both cats to relax. After this control period, it is a good idea to offer a special food treat (lightly microwaved mincemeat or tuna) to both cats.

3 If all has gone well, place both cats in their crates in the introduction room and position them side by side. After 5–10 minutes, calmly open the doors and allow them to leave (if they wish) and explore the room. If one or both returns to its crate, especially if there is any hissing or spitting, keep the door closed for another 10–15 minutes. If there is aggression at this stage, crate the established cat and remove it to another room. Allow 1–2 hours for the new cat to settle back down in the introduction room.

BELOW Feral cats will wander much further afield than domestic cats, seeking out food wherever they can find it.

These first three steps should be repeated over 4–5 days, until any anxiety or aggressive display has been reduced to acceptable levels. After each session, offer the cats some special food or treats within the crates as a reward. If they accept each other, place treats inside the crates with open doors.

4 This stage would be required only if acute aggression has occurred. In this instance, it is a good idea to use a harness for any cat that wants to fight while repeating the above steps. In this way, it is possible gradually to decrease the distance between the cats while maintaining full control over each individual.

It is important not to rush any of the stages, as failure could increase feline distress. These controlled stages are unnecessary if feline socialization is achieved naturally.

Do feral cats have a greater territory range than pet cats?

The few studies that have been undertaken have shown that the feral cat has a much wider range than the house cat. In some instances, especially with feral cats in rural environments, the difference can be significant and up to 30 times greater. Few feral cats will have been neutered, which means most toms are sexually active and driven to seek out queens with which to mate. The feral cat also rarely has the opportunity to enjoy a ready-made meal, so will usually have to travel much further afield than a domesticated cat to find food.

How can I stop another cat coming into my garden?

Apart from constructing a cat-proof netting cover that goes over the entire garden, there is little you can do. To prevent any cat from entering an open garden is extremely difficult unless you are prepared to lie in wait for it during a 24-hour period armed with a water-spray gun to dissuade it.

It is kinder and possibly easier to leave a number of cups (made from the bases of cut-down drinks bottles) containing human male urine around the perimeter walls, fences and flower beds. This method is based on the idea that a trespassing cat will believe that a giant, all-powerful cat has marked the garden as his. There is some anecdotal evidence that this method can have a short-term effect on possible intruders.

How can I stop my cat climbing on kitchen work surfaces?

One common method of preventing this behaviour is to spray the cat with water as it jumps up onto the work surface. However, this can lead to mistrust between cat and owner if the pet can associate the event with the human.

It is possible to use the combination of the clicker as a reward (see page 166) and training discs as a non-reward (see page 164) to help train your cat not to climb on kitchen work surfaces. If this training is started at the kitten stage it can be extremely effective.

When your cat leaps onto the work top, which it has learned to associate with food from its early days, sound the training discs. As soon as the cat jumps off and drops to the floor, sound the clicker and offer a food treat. The cat will soon learn that on the floor means food reward, whereas on the kitchen work surface means no food reward.

This training technique can only work in your presence, of course, although leaving the training discs hanging so that they are near the area where the cat jumps up may act as a further deterrent in your absence.

What are sensor sprays?

These are aerosol canisters that have a motion sensor included in the top. When a cat climbs onto a table or work surface, or approaches an area where marking behaviour is being displayed, the sensor picks up the movement and makes an audible signal. If the cat ignores this warning sound signal then the aerosol comes into action and gives out a short burst of a strong citronella scent that will surprise the cat.

Because the sensor detects the cat's movements and operates when you are absent, it can help to dissuade a cat from climbing onto work surfaces or spraying in a particular place without your intervention. By association with the strong smell, this aversion method will discourage the cat from undesirable behaviours without fostering any mistrust between the cat and the owner.

What are plug-in diffusers and how do they work?

This relatively new development in feline behaviour works on the same principle as a plug-in air freshener. However, instead of wafting a pleasant scent into the home, it sends out feline maternal pheromones. The device can be refilled as the reservoir empties. This may have a calming effect on the cat following installation, but long-term use suggests that it is not enough on its own to help cats with behaviour problems. Cats experiencing acute behavioural conditions may not benefit significantly from the use of these plug-in devices until a behavioural therapy has also been introduced to look after the problem.

Can a pheromone aerosol prevent a cat from spraying in the house?

Unfortunately, no. The idea behind an artificial pheromone spray is that it replaces a cat's natural facial scent-marking and is sprayed onto a target for inappropriate feline 'marking'. This could be an electrical plug (see page 171), toaster (see page 171), curtains or furniture. The principle on which this product is based is that the cat will not mark a target it believes it has marked already. However, it has been found that the use of this spray usually just redirects the cat to mark another target – and it is not practical to spray the entire house.

How do I know if my cat is contented?

There are a number of signs to look for.
The following will tell you whether or
not you have a happy cat:

- At some times of day you will not know
  that you have a cat, because it is
  snoozing in a favourite cupboard or
  sunning itself in the window.
- Your cat will use the litter tray or the
  garden at all times.
- It will scratch on its scratching post
  when the mood takes it.
- It will wander in and out of the home
  apparently without a care in the world.
- Your happy cat will stroll around the
  home, brushing up against a leg and
  sitting happily on the top edge of the
  sofa back without needing to jump into
  your lap every five minutes.
- It will eat regularly.

A contented cat is a joy to keep – but it
takes all types of personalities to make
the feline world go round.

Do cats suffer from 'separation anxiety' problems, just like children?

**Feline 'separation-related disorder' in
nervous cats is similar to the 'separation
anxiety' that some children (or even
adults) may develop.** There are several
known triggers for the onset of this
condition in nervous cats that have made
a powerful attachment to their owner.
These factors include:

- Physical and emotional trauma.
- Changes in the owner's work patterns.

- Sudden absence of the owner.
- House moves.
- Loss of a family member (human
  or feline).
- Infirmity.

Cats that have been through one or more
of these experiences are usually very
demanding of their owners and will seek
constant interaction with them in a
behaviour development known as
attention-seeking.

One or more of three main 'behaviour
signs' can be displayed when the cat is
separated from the owner. These are:

- Constant crying.
- Spraying and toileting inappropriately.
- Obsessive scratch-marking of furniture
  and doors.

Although these problem behaviours
usually occur when the cat is left alone,
they can sometimes be displayed even
when people are in the home but are
asleep or in a different room.

The length of time for which the cat is
left alone is unimportant. In rare cases,
the same behaviours can also be shown
when family members are around and
this may disguise or conceal the true
nervous condition.

If you want to know how your cat
behaves when separated from you,
consider filming it. Place a camcorder or
digital video camera on a tripod and
leave it running while you go through all
the motions of leaving the cat. Displays
or sounds that indicate the cat is
anxious, and vocalizations including
crying, may be recorded and this
information can provide an indication as
to if and to what degree the condition is
suffered by your cat.

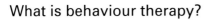

What is behaviour therapy?

Animal behavioural psychologists study and work with all animals, while working mainly with companion dogs and/or cats. They have studied animal behaviour and understand (with some limitations) how and why psychological problems develop in companion pets. Those with formal study experience understand the difference between genetically based behaviours (innate behaviour) and learned experiences that can have effects on both psychological behaviour and development.

Animal behavioural psychologists (known to scientists as ethologists) have worked with veterinary surgeons for several decades to develop behaviour therapies. These therapies will usually help owners to deal with antisocial behavioural problems that their pets have acquired, such as aggression, inappropriate indoor urinating and defecating, spraying, and withdrawal or feline depression, among other issues.

The animal behaviourist usually brings together both study and clinical experience (dealing with problem behaviour in cats on a regular basis) and counsels the owner on how best to deal with problems.

The pet therapy will often include guidance on handling, advice on feeding and recommendations about how to improve interaction between the owner and cat. These, together with clinically reviewed methods for countering the 'emotional' problems that lead a cat to display behavioural problems in the first place, are usually discussed in the home

of the cat and client. Perhaps ironically, most 'problem' behaviours are not antisocial in feline terms and in a natural environment, and from the cat's point of view are often the most instinctive outlets for dealing with life's ups and downs.

When applied by experts and put into action by caring cat owners, behavioural therapy is usually extremely successful at sorting out feline problems.

Is it *really* possible to train a cat?

Yes, if the targets for which you are aiming are realistic. Through 'reward and contact', cats can learn to:
• Come when called.
• Hunt for hidden toys and food treats.
• Jump up at targets.
• React to sounds.
Cats are perfectly capable of learning to associate actions, smells, sounds, movements and images with events in a process that is scientifically known as 'instrumental learning'.

They also learn through repeated association with one or more stimuli in a process that is known as 'classical conditioning' – open a tin of cat food and a conditioned response will occur in most cats (see page 145).

Unlike dogs, cats are not pack or social animals. Because of this fundamental difference, dogs are directly trainable for retrieval and agility work whereas cats have obvious limitations in these areas. However, healthy and happy cats do enjoy interactive play and most of their

ABOVE **Cats respond well to training with food and attention rewards to promote positive interaction with their owners.**

What is trial-and-error learning?

Trial-and-error learning is where, immediately or eventually, a cat learns how to escape from confinement or danger; when, where and how to obtain food or attention; and how to avoid competition, dangers and the wrong food types. Some of the earliest psychological experiments with cats revealed that, by trying various physical options, they could eventually learn to claw down a lever, push aside a swinging door and find a way out of the problem. Eventually, with the cat's combination of instinct, persistence and determination, 'trial and error' learning usually succeeds.

Can a cat really know its name and what its owner is saying to it?

A cat cannot know its name in the sense of understanding what its name is about or what it means. However, cats do learn that the sound of their given name, such as 'Charlie', has a phonetic ring to it. So the CH and the LEE in the name, when used on a daily basis, soon becomes associated with feeding time, play or contact, just as the call from a litter mother means that the kitten should reunite with her. Cats can learn by the sound of words, and associate each word with particular human actions and events. Owners are often ritualistic and repetitive in their daily life, and cats soon learn that certain words mean the likelihood of associated events occurring.

hunting techniques are learned in this way, first with their litter mother and then with their owner.

Cats are also capable of learning to perform behaviours in order to get what they want. So, through the use of food rewards and attention rewards, it is possible for a owners to condition their cats to perform behaviours or to recall to a name, but any more complex training than this probably requires more effort than most cats and owners will be prepared to spend.

What is the best way to 'call' my cat to encourage it home at night?

It is advisable to establish a signal other than just a name call from the earliest days of owning a cat. This signal – which could be the sound of a tinkling bell, a spoon tapped on a food dish or even a whistle – would precede any name call. Once a cat strongly associates with this sound, usually after a week or so, it can be used to recall the cat if it should ever wander off or become lost. The simple sound, used repeatedly, will carry further into the night air and is not as complicated as a name call.

Why should I use clicker training with my cat?

Clicker training (see page 166) harnesses 'positive reinforcement' methods to reward ideal behaviour from companion animals and has proved hugely successful with cats. Cats quickly 'understand', or rather learn to make the association between the unique double-click sound that the small plastic device makes and an established link to a food reward together with pleasurable contact with their owner.

Once a cat has made this mental association, the sound can then be used to praise a cat for good behaviour, to play games of hiding foods (the clicker is sounded for success), and for rewarding recall to another sound signal that would initially encourage a cat to return home when necessary.

Why should I use training discs with my cat?

The use of training discs, much better known as a dog-training aid, is relatively new with cats. This device is a set of symbols not unlike those on a tambourine, on a short thread that create a distinctive sound when shaken.

Once the sound of the discs has been conditioned into the cat's subconscious and become associated with either the removal or denial of a food treat (see page 164), they can be sounded gently to signal and interrupt any potential problem behaviours.

This will be more effective than shouted word instructions (such as 'Off!' or 'Stop!') and will not promote the problem behaviour in the way that the owner's attention does.

Should I use the clicker system to help train my cat to use the litter tray?

Positive-association or reward methods have a long and successful record in training animals. Very few animals, including humans, fail to respond to a method that rewards good behaviour. Every time the cat uses the litter tray and is therefore clean around the house, the clicker can be sounded to signal that this behaviour will trigger a food reward.

A cat will obviously want to trigger a food reward from its owner and so, by subconscious association, will learn to perform the behaviour that elicits the treat.

Should I use the clicker system to help train my cat to use a scratching post?

ABOVE Cats naturally want to scratch posts but if they need encouragement then try using cat nip or the clicker system.

First the cat must be trained to associate the sound of the clicker with a food treat (see page 166). Then, sounding the clicker as the cat uses the scratching post will encourage it to repeat the behaviour.

The 'positive reinforcement' of the use of the scratching post will help to ensure your cat uses this instead of furniture, interior objects and doors.

8

Reproduction

Can you sex kittens by looking at them?

Kittens that are between the ages of 6 and 24 weeks can be difficult to sex visually, unless you have experience in breeding cats. Professional breeders have little problem with working out this difference, because they have the experience to know how to compare young toms and queens almost from the day they were born.

With more than one kitten and both genders to consider, a visual comparison can be made, which can make the differences obvious.

Lift up the kitten's tail to observe the anal area. The female's anus (upper opening) and vulva (lower opening) are in line, one directly above the other and are quite close to each other. This closeness is quite distinctive.

By contrast, the male's anal opening (again at the top) is in line with his testicles (just beneath) and with his penis farther down. However, the testicles and penis will be under-developed at the early kitten stage.

In contrast, adult cats can be sexed very easily from behind because in most breeds the testicles of the males are highly visible.

ABOVE RIGHT The male kitten has a scrotal sac beneath its anal opening.

RIGHT The female kitten's vulva opening is immediately below the anal opening.

Do I really need to get my cat neutered?

Unless you are intending to use your cat for breeding purposes, the answer is a resounding 'yes'. A pair of 'entire' or un-neutered cats, left to roam, mate and hunt freely, could be the source of hundreds of unwanted kittens within 12 months. Neutering will prevent this unwelcome outcome.

It will also prevent any other unwanted matings that could occur in a house cat that is exposed to the outdoor cat population. Cats are naturally secretive and mainly nocturnal animals, and it can be an eye-opening exercise to view the true local cat population when walking around your home area at night. This is especially true in densely human-populated urban areas, where cat numbers can be extraordinarily high.

Castration or spaying of a kitten before 6 months of age will reduce the chances of it marking in the home. When these surgical operations are performed on adult cats (commonly in adopted cats), they rarely alter or stop indoor marking behaviours without a behavioural therapy in place.

Will neutering change a tom's personality?

A neutered tom will undergo a significant personality change. However, this process can depend on the age at which the neutering is performed. Early neutering at or before 6 months of age will have less effect than a later operation and hormone levels will take much longer to subside in an older cat.

A young kitten will barely have developed male behaviours when castration occurs. This means that there is less likelihood of spraying and aggressive behaviours occurring. In contrast, an adult cat will already have matured sexually and will often continue to display marking behaviours and independence even after neutering.

Neutered toms usually patrol and protect a more modest territory beyond the home. Interaction with the owner is often less volatile and more predictable. A neutered tom can eventually become more clingy and home loving.

Will neutering change a queen's personality?

Just as age dictates how a tom's personality will change with neutering (see left), the same applies to queens. A young female kitten may show a tendency to follow her owner around, as hormones that would influence maturity and sexual behaviour diminish. She will also be less likely to display such unwanted habits as spraying or aggressive behaviour in later life.

A neutered female adult, reacting adversely to the trauma of intrusive surgery that is greater for her than for a male, usually becomes more bonded with her owner and will show little desire to wander beyond the home territory. Neutered females are said to be healthier, more likely to be affectionate and more contented than entire cats.

Will neutering change the sexual behaviour of my tom?

Although still male in brain and body, the neutered tom will rarely express the urge to seek out queens and will experience a significant reduction in his desire to roam. He will feel a reduced drive to mark his territory with urine, although nervousness in neutered males will often result in spraying behaviour.

Will neutering change the sexual behaviour of my queen?

A young kitten will not have had time to interact sexually with male cats. In this case, neutering simply prevents the development of sexually driven behaviour. A neutered older queen remains female in body and brain and may still express a desire to be among other cats, even though she is less likely to compete with them over territory. She will not experience the hormone-driven urge to mate.

ABOVE Neutering does not affect a cat's aggressive tendences. Neutered cats are just as likely to display aggression as entire or unneutered cats.

How do other cats view a neutered tom?

Other neutered cats will certainly be aware of the gender of a neutered tom. This is because his 'maleness' will not change and testosterone levels, while reduced by castration, will still confirm his sex. The degree of hormonal signals will be reduced and the neutered male is much less of a threat to others, although territorial aggression can still remain uppermost in his and another cat's mind.

How do other cats view a neutered queen?

A female cat that has been spayed might be seen as neutral by other cats. However, her oestrogen levels, while reduced by the effects of neutering, will ensure she is still regarded as a female by male cats. If a female is territorially aggressive, neutering will not eradicate this behaviour.

There are accounts of toms attempting to mate with neutered females, but in the majority of cases they are not seen as potential mating conquests by entire male cats.

- Possible treatment costs (for any complications at or following birth).
- Advertising costs.
- Extra food costs.
- Veterinary fees (for routine worming and vaccinations).
- Time (spent supporting the litter mother and dealing with her offspring).

What do I need to take into account if I wish to breed my cat?

The most important and daunting task facing the owner of non-pedigree kittens is how to find good, safe homes for them. In contrast, because there is a fee to be paid, owners of pedigree kittens will usually find dedicated cat lovers to give them good homes.

Other factors to consider before allowing a queen to be mated include:

When do young cats become fertile?

Young males reach puberty and begin sexual development at about 6 months of age. Young females begin 'calling' (giving out a constant series of cries to

BELOW Cats can be sexually active from an early age and should be neutered before they reach six months old. Siamese and Burmese cats mature sexually before other breeds.

attract males) when they begin their first season, at between 5 and 7 months of age. It is reported that some long-haired females can be as old as 10 months before they become fertile and that the actual age at which a female cat becomes fertile is dependent on the breed.

A mature female cat can have up to three litters in a year, and so can produce up to about 18 kittens in that period.

What do I do when an accidental mating occurs?

The first stages of pregnancy in a female cat can go unnoticed. Often it is only when the cat's underbelly becomes visibly extended after five weeks' gestation that the situation is recognized. If it is known that an accidental mating has occurred, your veterinary surgeon

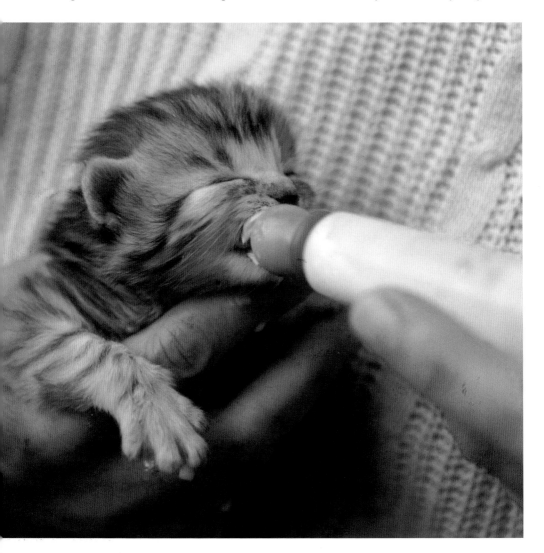

LEFT **Hand-rearing kittens interferes with their natural socialization. Kittens isolated from other cats never completely learn normal cat behaviour.**

ABOVE **A female cat's pregnant underbelly can be the first sign of gestation. This is clearly visible after five weeks. Gestation in cats lasts for around 65 days.**

may be able to abort the kittens within 48 hours, but this is rarely undertaken when health risks and the danger of introducing infection to the pregnant female are taken into consideration.

Gestation in cats lasts for around 65 days, and within this time you will need to obtain or make a kittening box. This should be partially covered, to offer the litter mother the security that she would seek out from a secure bolt hole. The pregnant queen will need an enhanced diet to ensure that she has all the nutrients that she needs and that both she and her unborn kittens are in good health and ready for the birth.

Is it possible to hand-rear a kitten without problems occurring?

With much dedication and constant care, it is possible to hand-rear a kitten. There are situations, such as when the litter mother has gone missing and the kittens are found apparently abandoned, when a newborn kitten may need to be nurtured by the owner or other concerned person. However, this is known to lead to behavioural problems in later life. The removal of a kitten during the litter stages interrupts important developments in socialization and learning from the litter mother.

Can cats miscarry?

It is possible for a pregnant queen to miscarry. This would normally indicate sexual immaturity or infirmity, stress, foetal abnormality or an infection in the womb (uterus) region. It is known that foetal mortality in the early weeks of pregnancy can result in their reabsorption by the cat.

Can other cats tell when my cat is ready to breed?

Other cats will be aware of a queen coming into season from quite a distance away. This is achieved through hormonal scent signals and the queen 'calling', which includes constant cries, and physical behaviours such as rolling and exposing the underbelly.

Do I take my cat to another cat to have her mated?

You can contact a breeder through professional registers or your local veterinary surgery. You will need to discuss breed standards to ensure that any resulting kittens measure up and will therefore find good homes. You will also need to talk about the fee structure, and then arrange to have your queen mated.

An alternative for an owner with a non-pedigree cat would be simply to get in touch with another cat owner with an entire male and arrange for the two cats to come into contact with each other when your queen is in season.

How do I use my male cat as a sire?

This situation will normally arise only if you have a pedigree cat. A rare form, of a breed much sought after by others is most likely to interest owners who wish to breed their queens.

The first step towards using your tom for breeding would be to contact the secretary of the local cat club and arrange to go along to a local cat show. In this environment, it should be possible to meet other cat owners and discuss the pedigree breeding standards that are applicable to your breed and the viability of your cat as a sire.

How can I tell if my cat is pregnant?

There are several telltale signs to look for. These develop at different stages of gestation:
- The earliest point at which you will be able to tell is between 14 and 21 days after mating. Close examination of the pregnant female's nipples will reveal that they are slightly enlarged and pink, and this is an early indication that she has kittens on the way.
- Later on, the ventral or belly area will show signs of enlargement and the underbelly fur may appear more dense than usual.
- During the 30- to 40-day period, it should become more obvious from the weight gain and distended belly that your cat is carrying kittens towards full term, at 60–65 days.

How long does a cat pregnancy last?

The average period between a cat being impregnated and birth is about 65 days. Birth can occur anywhere between 60 and 70 days, depending on the breed and the individual cat.

How can I tell when my cat is ready to give birth?

The queen's breathing rate will increase and early occasional contractions can be seen rippling through her underbelly. This phase can take anything between 4 and 8 hours.

As the kittens, which are enclosed in individual fluid-filled birth sacs, travel towards and into the birth canal, the contractions increase until they are only seconds apart before the kittens begin to be expelled. This phase lasts between 20 minutes and 1 hour, but should take no longer than 90 minutes.

Should I stay with my cat as she gives birth?

It can be useful for you to monitor the fluctuating birth situation from a short distance away from the kittening box, but do not fuss or try to handle her. In this way, you will be able to detect complications as early as possible. If there are signs of distress and difficulty during the final birthing stages, you will need to contact your veterinary surgeon as quickly as you can.

Do I need to ask a veterinary surgeon to attend the birth?

Unless the kittens are at risk or potentially extremely valuable, this is unnecessary. Most feline births take place perfectly satisfactorily without professional supervision.

What if there are complications at the birth?

There are a couple of 'complications' in which you can intervene to help the kittens and/or the litter mother.
- Most kittens are born head first, but many can be born tail first (breech). This is not really a complication, but in some instances you may need to encourage the cat with a helping hand if a kitten seems stuck part-way out.
- When kittens are born but the litter mother hasn't released them from their birth sacs, you can help by doing this for her, then rubbing them gently with a warm towel and wiping them around the nose, ears and eyes to clear any possible blockages caused by the fluid.

Any complications that are clearly causing the litter mother distress should be dealt with by a veterinary surgeon.

What is a 'phantom pregnancy'?

Occasionally a queen may develop all the signs of pregnancy but without the obvious physical developments. This condition, known as pseudo-pregnancy

or phantom pregnancy, is caused by hormonal imbalances or after mating with a sterile tom. It is often combined with stress-induced behaviours and this can lead to a phantom pregnancy. The queen can begin to care for phantom kittens and will show all her maternal drive towards inanimate objects such as soft toys. It is often best to allow her to perform the motions of maternal behaviour and come through this feline post-natal process naturally.

Can a pregnant cat still be given vaccinations?

Most vaccinations are contra-indicated in pregnant animals because of the possible risks of harm to the kittens. Litter mothers should be vaccinated either before getting pregnant or immediately after birth.

Are worming and flea treatments safe for a pregnant cat?

Most of these treatments are safe for a cat during pregnancy. Nevertheless, veterinary surgeons would only recommend those where data is available to show they are safe to use during pregnancy, so it is always best to check with a professional first.

LEFT **A nesting box should be comfortable and make your cat feel safe. This nesting box has been lined with a towel and makes an ideal kittening environment.**

Do I need to give the litter mother a special diet during pregnancy and after birth?

Any dietary support will help a litter mother to build up her physical and emotional strength through the pre- and post-natal periods.

Specially formulated vitamin and mineral supplements can be added to the standard food or special feline diets can be given to help a pregnant queen. These additives or superior complete diets will also help provide the correct nutrients for the growth of the unborn kittens (via the placenta) and of the youngsters once they are in the world (via the litter mother's milk).

How do I confine the litter mother and kittens?

A kittening box placed in a quiet part of the home is essential if the litter mother is to be comfortable during the birth process. The box can be a purpose-built wooden unit or a strong, converted cardboard box with both open and closed-off sections to create the covered nest effect.

What items do I need for the kittening box?

There are just a few essential items for a kittening box.
- Old towels, to be destroyed after the birth and replaced.
- Fleece or warm towelling, for bedding.

- Newspapers or disposable bedding, for the toileting area.
- Suspended infra red or heat lamp (if the room is cold)

How many kittens does a litter mother give birth to?

The average number of kittens in a litter is six. There are records of single kittens being born, as well as litters of eight.

BELOW **The average size of a litter is six kittens. A mature cat can have up to three litters a year – a total of 18 kittens.**

What do I do with the kittens when they are first born?

Unless there have been complications with the birth, there is not a great deal you need to do. Your main responsibility is to offer the litter mother good food, plenty of peace and quiet, and warmth for her offspring.

Can I handle the newborn kittens right away?

This is not usually necessary or desirable. However, if the kittens are particularly messy you can gently wipe them down

with a cloth soaked in lukewarm water and then towel dry with a warm, soft baby towel. Do not handle the kittens excessively, as this might disturb the routine of the litter mother. Occasional brief handling of the kittens – say, every other day – will help to condition and socialize them to human touch.

What is the 'reflex' period for kittens?

Kittens are born blind and deaf, and are cared for totally by the litter mother. The first weeks of their life are known as the reflex period, during which the mother will constantly groom the kittens and offer her teats to them for sustenance.

ABOVE **Kittens are born blind and deaf and rely on instinct and the litter mothers' care. They open their eyes when they are between 2 and 10 days old.**

What do newborn kittens eat?

The litter mother supplies her newborn kittens with nothing more than her milk. This essential food, which is naturally provided by a healthy litter mother, contains everything that they need in order to develop in the first few weeks.

What does the term 'weaning' mean?

The weaning period is when the kittens can be introduced to more solid food, and begin to be 'weaned' off their mother's milk. This takes place between 3 and 4 weeks, as they start to take their first real steps under the litter mother's supervision. At first the kittens will take a combination of their mother's milk and food that is the consistency of babyfood, but by the time they are 4 or 5 weeks old they will happily eat finely chopped-up, solid food. In this period they will start to expend more energy, as they get brave enough to explore outside the nest area or box, begin to cross thresholds and peep through open doors.

When the kittens are weaned, what should I feed them?

Once the weaning period has been accomplished and the kittens are suckling less intensively, you can start to feed them. The now active and naturally inquisitive kittens can be offered semi-solid meals of mashed-up sardines, finely blended mincemeat and finely chopped proprietary kitten food.

In natural conditions in the wild, kittens at this stage of development are able to take some regurgitated food from their mother, and will soon be able to take small meals from the prey which she brings back to them.

BELOW Weaning starts with small single meals to supplement the mothers' milk. By 8 to 9 weeks kittens are ready for regular cat food.

How much food do the weaned kittens need?

During weaning, begin with a small, single meal to supplement the litter mother's milk. This is because a kitten's stomach is tiny and you do not want to overload it. Gradually increase this until the kittens are eating between three and six small meals per day at 6 weeks old.

By about 8 or 9 weeks, the fast-developing kittens will be able to eat standard cat food and will thrive on good quality brands. (For more details on kitten diets, see page 98.)

Why is the litter mother thin and very hungry all the time?

The mother's instinct drives her, above all else, to provide the milk that is essential for her kittens (cat's milk is nearly twice as rich as cow's milk). She puts her own needs second, in a perfect example of maternal behaviour. Providing kittens with a constant supply of nutritious milk on demand drains her physical resources.

How many times should the litter mother be fed each day?

It is highly important to offer the litter mother several small meals spread across the day. You should allow her to eat as much as she wants during each session, then remove any food that she has not wanted to eat.

She should also have a constant source of clean water that is best drawn off in bottles and allowed to stand overnight. This makes it more attractive to her, because the chlorine content will naturally diminish as the water rises to room temperature.

Is it normal for a litter mother to abandon her kittens?

It is not usual behaviour, but there are instances of litter mothers leaving their firstborn kittens after the nest area has been disturbed. There may also be instances where the litter mother is immature and has not quite developed the instinct to look after her charges. In some cases, the missing litter mother has simply gone hunting to provide for herself and her offspring, and events have overtaken her task. This could be aggression from other cats or, in urban settings, trauma from a road traffic accident or similar incident.

A litter mother that cannot wait to get back into her old ways of prowling and defending her territory will show much less interest in her developing kittens from about 5 or 6 weeks.

Does the male cat help to care for the kittens?

The male cat plays no active role in caring for the kittens. However, in nature he would be fighting territorial battles with rival males, and this behaviour could have the secondary effect of protecting the fragile kittens from a marauding tom cat that might just fancy kitten for dinner or to destroy another cat's offspring.

Should you let your female cat breed at least once?

There is a myth in cat (and dog) ownership that it is more natural for females to breed at least once in their lifetime. However, evidence suggests there is nothing lost in a queen (or a bitch) not having a litter and some veterinary surgeons might argue that less stress on the physical well-being of the cat will help her to fight off disease and illness through her life.

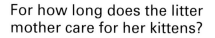
For how long does the litter mother care for her kittens?

This may vary, depending on the degree of maternal drive the litter mother naturally displays. A litter mother with a strong maternal instinct will care for her kittens throughout the 9 or 10 weeks of their early kittenhood, usually until her milk begins to dry up. In nature, this mother would almost guarantee a perfect start to life, and natural selection will have succeeded.

BELOW A litter mother carries one of her kittens from the nesting site to a safe area. She carries them, one by one, holding them by the scruff of the neck.

How many litters can a cat have and stay healthy?

Queens can produce litters throughout their lifetime, as there is no feline equivalent of the human menopause. However, if a litter mother were to have pregnancies throughout her life, she would be physically drained and open to major organ diseases and conditions. Most breeders would argue for the ideal of an adult litter mother having five to seven years of no more than one or two litters per year.

Can a queen be infertile?

Some queens have been recorded as being unable to conceive and are considered infertile. In most cases where this occurs, the cat has suffered a uterine or vaginal infection that prevents her from mating successfully.

Should a kitten have started its vaccinations before it goes to a new home?

A kitten's series of vaccinations should start at around 8 weeks of age. So, the answer to the question depends on the age of the kitten when it is first homed (see page 88). Professional breeders, who usually release kittens at between 10 and 12 weeks old, will usually provide a vaccination certificate that may include records of one or two sessions. The vaccines are usually given a month apart, and it is vital that a kitten is not allowed

ABOVE **Your veterinary surgeon will advise on the vaccinations necessary for your kitten. Courses of injections start at about 8 weeks.**

outside the home or to come into contact with other cats during this period. If there is any doubt about the current vaccination situation, it is best for the new owner to err on the side of caution and assume that it is necessary to start the vaccinations immediately.

Should kittens be wormed before they go to a new home?

A professional breeder begins worming the kittens to protect them against roundworms at 6 or 7 weeks of age. Any kitten taken for adoption will usually have been wormed. Kittens can be treated for potential tapeworm infestation at 6 months.

Health

9

How can I tell if my cat is healthy and happy?

This is easy. If your cat's behaviour doesn't change dramatically overnight, and eating and activity habits remain regular and normal, there's a good chance that there is nothing at all to worry about (see page 187).

A happy and healthy cat will have been properly socialized and cared for as a kitten both by the breeder and you as an owner. In adult life, the cat will undergo as few home changes as possible and experience little, if any, stress.

The first sign of physical problems will usually be an obvious indication that something has changed for the worse. A cat that:
• is breathing badly
• is moving about awkwardly
• or remains unusually inactive
should be examined by a vet as soon as possible. These physical changes immediately suggest that an injury has been sustained by the cat, or that there is an internal organ breakdown or infection (see also page 217).

A cat that suddenly changes its personality, transforming from outgoing to withdrawn behaviour, is unhappy or unsettled about some factor in its life. For a list of possible causes, see opposite.

ABOVE **If a cat looks in good shape, is lively and full of play and curiosity, then it is likely to be healthy and happy.**

How can I maintain my cat's health?

A cat that has had an excellent start in life is ideally equipped to fight off most of the physical tests that nature may offer. There are several factors involved. The cat will have:
• Started life physically healthy.
• Been fully vaccinated against the common feline infections, wormed and treated for fleas.
• Enjoyed a balanced and varied diet.
• Been encouraged to be independent and active.
With this in place, there is little reason – beyond the unexpected – why your cat should not lead a long and healthy life.

Play, stalking, play-hunting, prowling and exploration behaviours are important to a young cat and you should encourage such activities. An active cat is usually a happy cat – this aspect may actually be the most important factor in a healthy cat's lifestyle.

Stress and physical trauma will take their toll on any cat, but the healthier it is to begin with, the better able it will be to overcome the trials and tribulations that occur during its life.

What factors are known to cause stress in cats?

Many of the factors that are known to cause stress in humans can have the same effect on cats. Significant changes that are known to trigger stress-related behaviours in companion cats include:

- House moves – because cats are territorial.
- Introduction or loss of cats within a territory – for the same reason.
- Changes in ownership – because relationship attachments or bonds are broken.
- Trauma – physical, such as being attacked, intrusive surgery, illness or injury; or psychological, such as aggression from another cat.
- Changes in the owner's lifestyle, such as work or home patterns – because cats like consistency and routine.
- Temporary or permanent loss of a family member – because, again, relationship bonds are broken.
- A new person staying in the home or the arrival of a baby – because both bring a huge array of new scents into the home.

ABOVE Cats can become very withdrawn in the same way that humans can, when they are experiencing stress or are unhappy, .

How can I tell if my cat is stressed or unhappy?

There are a number of signs that an owner can look for. A stressed or unhappy cat may:

- Begin to groom itself excessively or obsessively.
- Sometimes become withdrawn and unaffectionate towards it owner.
- Become agoraphobic and refuse completely to leave the house, where once it wanted to explore its territory on a daily basis.
- Lose its appetite, although this change in behaviour is more likely to be linked to physical disorders.

A cat showing any of these symptoms is unhappy with its current situation.

Unusual behaviour, especially inactivity and hiding away.

Loss of appetite.

Weight loss.

Excessive grooming.

Excessive drinking of water.

Regurgitation of food.

Difficulty breathing.

Loose stools.

Cloudy eyes.

Poor balance.

Awkward movement.

Excessive vocalization.

Refusal to leave the house when normally keen to do so.

ABOVE Refer to the list of signs of illness or stress, right, if there are any doubts about a kitten's well-being.

How can I tell if my cat is unwell?

The first indication that a cat is unwell is usually that its normal behaviour patterns change. This might mean an active cat becomes inactive; sleeping more and eating less. There can be more obvious indications of poor health in the cat's physical appearance, movements or locomotion, which change from stealth-like to clumsy or awkward.

Signs to look for are summarized in the table above. Once the early signs of ill-health are detected it is advisable to consult your veterinary surgeon as soon as possible so that an illness can be dealt with before it becomes serious.

How can I tell if my cat is nervous?

It is fairly easy to judge whether or not your cat is nervous. A nervous cat will disappear upstairs to a known bolt hole, such as underneath a bed or in a secluded cupboard, as soon as a visitor enters its owner's home. Healthy cats are naturally inquisitive and would normally want to mark or brush up against a newcomer to the home to express their possessiveness. A cat that is anxious will not interact with visitors (or sometimes, even its owner) in the way a confident companion pet would in this respect.

Are there any cross-infections or health risks involved in keeping a cat?

Any owner or family member with asthma would be at risk when keeping a cat. However, despite the possibility of cat hair around a person with asthma triggering an attack, it could be argued that the positive psychological aspects of stroking and interacting with a companion animal outweigh the negative physical effects.

It is known that Toxoplasma (dangerous to pregnant women), ringworm, Salmonella and, most serious of all, rabies, can all be contracted from cats. If a veterinary surgeon isolates some strains of Salmonella from a sample taken from a cat under treatment, they may have a legal obligation to inform you (depending on jurisdiction).

The most unlikely (yet still possible) cross-infection would result from an owner accidentally swallowing a cat flea, which could lead to tapeworm infection in the person.

Is weight loss in cats a serious condition?

Abrupt weight loss in cats indicates a serious major organ disease or infection, or that a feline nervous condition has developed. Once a veterinary surgeon has eliminated any possible physical causes, it is important that the owner immediately consults an animal behaviourist who specializes in treating feline psychological disorders.

ABOVE A cat that repeatedly vomits may be showing symptoms of a serious illness or of having ingested some poison.

What is feline leukaemia?

Leukaemia is a disease of the blood. In this condition, the body cannot limit the production of white blood cells. These are vital to the immune system, but uncontrolled production can damage blood vessels and internal organs. In cats, viral feline leukaemia is transmissible through body fluids via mating or biting, and can be fatal. Diagnosis is made through blood analysis.

There is no treatment available for infected cats, although vaccinations given at 9 and 13 weeks can protect a cat (although they are not 100 percent effective). Some infected cats can recover from exposure to the virus and signs of the disease.

The common signs of infection are:

- Fever.
- Lethargy.
- Enlarged lymph nodes.
- Anaemia.
- Dramatic loss of appetite.
- Acute weight loss.

What is feline dysautonomia?

This is a rare disease which affects the nervous system and has a high mortality rate in cats that do become infected. It is also known as Key-Gaskell syndrome. The causes of this group of diseases are currently a mystery to the veterinary profession. However, the considered opinion is that it is linked to viral infections.

The signs of the disease are:

- Diluted pupils and third-eyelid protrusion.
- Dry mouth.
- Loss of appetite.
- Uncontrolled loss of body wastes.
- Vomiting.

It is reported that intensive care and gentle handling is required because swallowing is impeded by paralysis of the gullet. The condition must be closely monitored by a veterinary surgeon.

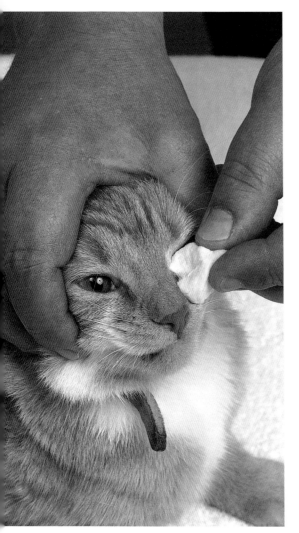

ABOVE Eye infections in cats can be limited to a number of serious feline infections. The eyes of a cat will often reflect its state of health.

survive infection, but they are potential carriers and should be isolated or euthanized. There is a possible 3-year incubation period following infection during which the cat may not show any

What is cat 'flu, or feline viral rhinotracheitis?

There is a high infection but low mortality rate in cats that contract viral rhinotracheitis. Fatalities can occur in older cats or those already suffering from other infections that depress the immune system. The signs of infection are:

• Coughing.
• Sneezing.
• Discharge from the nose.
• Loss of appetite.
• Withdrawn behaviour.

These are much the same symptoms suffered by humans who have been laid low by influenza.

Outbreaks are common in warm seasons when groups of cats come together or are housed in boarding catteries. An infected cat should be kept warm, dry, quiet and rested until it makes a full recovery.

What is feline calici virus?

This is one of several 'flu viral infections that has been identified in cats showing the signs of ear, nose and throat inflammation. An early sign of infection can be observed when a withdrawn cat begins to make a distinctive cough or bark and is not regurgitating a fur ball.

What does it mean when my cat coughs repeatedly?

Most commonly, a coughing cat is attempting to regurgitate a developing fur ball with its vomit. In other cases, the cat may have consumed grass in order to bring up a digestive irritation or fur ball. In rare cases, the coughing may be a sign of feline calici virus (see left). If you have

any suspicions that this may be the cause of your cat's coughing, veterinary help should be sought.

What could be causing my cat's eye infection?

There are a number of causes for eye infections in cats. It is advisable to first of all have the worst-case scenarios eliminated through professional examination. In some cases, the cat may have been exposed to bad weather, been the victim of aggression or in a chase with another cat or may have been caught in the eye by a branch or plant. In more serious cases, the infection is a sign of feline chlamydial disease (see below) and veterinary help should be sought immediately.

What is feline chlamydial disease?

This disease (common in young kittens up to 9 months old) is caused by a bacterial infection, *Chlamydia psittaci*, that attacks the eyes. Feline chlamydial is closely related to a disease found in tropical parrots.

The ailment is a form of conjunctivitis that results in discharge from the eyes and nose and often causes a cat to sneeze repeatedly. The infection is countered through the use of a course of antibiotics, which prevents possible infection in the digestive and reproductive systems. Young cats can be vaccinated against the disease.

ABOVE It is vital to have a sick cat examined by your veterinary surgeon at an early stage of an illness.

Why does my cat have trouble urinating?

There are a number of infections and conditions that might cause this problem. A common ailment in male cats is feline urological syndrome (see above right), while other cats may be suffering from infections of the bladder or urethra or have feline cystitis. You should consult a veterinary surgeon at the earliest opportunity to prevent further health complications resulting from the condition.

What is feline urological syndrome?

This condition, once common in cats fed only on complete dried foods, results in a blockage in the urethra in male cats. The combination of this diet, dehydration and early castration can lead to the formation of salt crystals in the bladder that block the urethra. A cat suffering from the effects of this condition will struggle to pass urine, which causes the bladder to expand and results in extreme pain. It is vital to arrange immediate treatment to alleviate the distress caused by this syndrome.

Is feline urological syndrome the same as feline cystitis?

Feline cystitis is a bladder inflammation that affects mainly female cats, and is sometimes associated with infection rather than a general condition related to other influences. The primary sign of this disease is an increase in the number of times urination is attempted, with an obvious reduction in the amount of urine passed. A secondary sign of infection can be blood in the urine. Although not life-threatening it is extremely uncomfortable for the cat. A veterinary surgeon will advise on a course of treatment.

What should I do when my cat has diarrhoea?

Some cats can shows signs of looseness that may be related to the consistency or

age of the last meal they have eaten. A cat that is showing signs of stress (see pages 213–214) may also have diarrhoea. Alternatively, it may simply be that the cat's digestive system needs to purge itself and careful feeding for 48 hours will see the end of the problem. However, repeated bouts of loose stools or diarrhoea should be investigated urgently. If a cat is also regurgitating, there could be a danger of rapid dehydration and serious health implications, including enteritis (see below).

There are also some serious parasitical and bacterial diseases, such as tapeworm, Campylobacter and Salmonella, that result in diarrhoea in cats and all these can be contracted by humans. It is wise to be extremely vigilant over hygiene, including using an antibacterial wash for your hands, and taking extra care when handling the cat and clearing up its faeces.

There can be many causes for prolonged diarrhoea in cats, including infections of the colon and feline infectious enteritis. These and other infections, infestations and conditions require urgent veterinary examination and laboratory tests.

What is feline infectious enteritis?

This is a potentially lethal infection that is highly contagious and can lead to mortality within a matter of hours. There is an incubation period of 2–9 days in which the intestines, liver and white blood cells are attacked. A cat that is infected with the disease will be hunched up rather than stretched out, and when its underbelly is examined it will react to the acute painfulness of the condition.

Intensive nursing care can sometimes result in recovery in an otherwise strong and healthy cat.

Can cats become anaemic?

Cats can suffer from anaemia. This occurs when there is a reduction in the number of red blood cells, normally associated with low iron content. There are a number of causes for anaemia in cats, including:
• Blood loss following injury.
• Cancer.
• Viral feline leukaemia.
• Infestation of internal/external parasites.
• Poisoning.
• Major organ disease.
• Inadequate diet.
Treatment varies and depends on diagnosing the cause.

What could have caused my cat to have a swollen underbelly?

Excessive or hanging fur and skin on the underbelly can be seen in neutered female cats that are fed almost entirely on dried food. The cat will gradually take on the appearance of being pregnant or overweight, but this is simply a sagging effect on the underbelly and should not cause concern. However, feline infectious peritonitus (see page 220), could also cause a sudden body-cavity swelling and this requires veterinary investigation.

Cats cannot be vaccinated against this disease and only isolation and treatment for secondary infections can be used. For all infectious diseases, check with your local veterinarian who will be able to tell you the most up-to-date information.

Why does my cat have bad breath?

There are a number of causes for bad breath in cats. The more obvious ones include decayed or infected teeth and feline gingivitis or gum infection. Otherwise it could be stomatitis (an inflammation of the mouth lining), an imbalance in the digestive system or a serious internal infection.

Regular teeth cleaning with cat toothpaste can help a cat that suffers from tooth and gum decay. You should get an acute mouth odour checked by a veterinary surgeon, not only to identify and treat the condition but also to prevent the possible development of secondary infections.

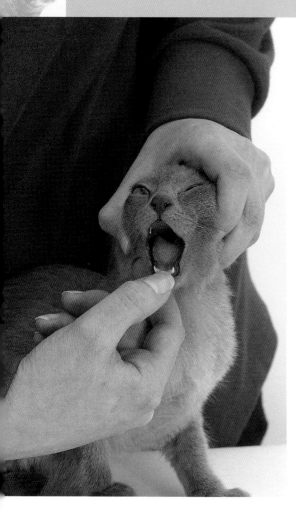

ABOVE **A close examination of a cat's mouth and teeth can often reveal signs of illness.**

What is feline infectious peritonitus?

This is a disease of the abdominal cavity that also affects the liver, kidneys and nervous system, including the brain. Young cats are particularly vulnerable. The main signs to be alert to are loss of appetite, raised temperature and fever, and an enlarged or swollen abdomen.

What is the temperature of a healthy cat?

The temperature of a calm, healthy cat is 38–39°C (100–102°F). A cat's temperature can be taken with a lubricated thermometer gently inserted into the rectum for about a minute. Lift the cat's tail up at the base and insert the small thermometer, then wipe it clean before reading. Only take a cat's temperature in this way if you are confident about handling and the procedure.

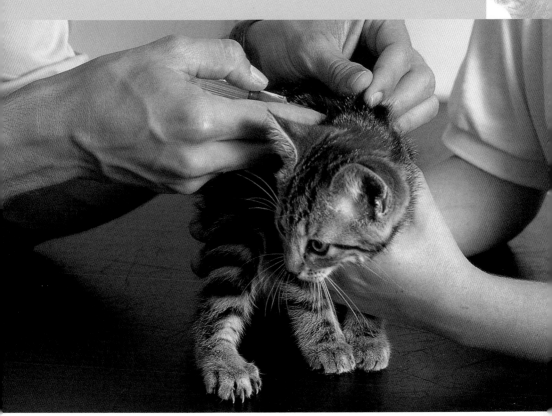

What vaccinations does my kitten need?

The range of vaccinations that a kitten requires often depends on the region where you live and what your veterinary surgeon may advise. Most kittens are immunized against the most serious and life-threatening feline diseases such as viral rhinotracheitis (see page 216).

Do cats really need booster injections?

There have been constant debates among professionals about the need for regular booster vaccinations. It has been argued that in the case of humans no boosters are

ABOVE It is essential for kittens to be immunized against serious feline diseases. Ask your veterinary surgeon what the kitten needs, and when.

given following the initial immunization, so why give them to cats (and dogs)? The theory is that the immune system makes its response and then the particular disease can be fought naturally. Others argue that, because cats and dogs can be exposed to the fluctuating risk of diseases and infections by coming into contact with animals carrying them, a regular booster is needed.

It is always advisable to discuss this with your veterinary surgeon, as they will be aware of the local situation as far as the incidence of infections is concerned.

Do I need to worm my cat?

It is necessary to worm a cat because of the debilitating effects of the parasite burden and the increased possibility of re-infection through the egg cycle. Cats that are infected with parasites will lose valuable energy and important nutrients. This factor, added to the pressure that major organs and the immune system come under as internal parasites develop, can bring untold stress on a cat.

How often should I worm my cat?

Ideally, an adult cat should be wormed every 6 months. If parasite infections are diagnosed, your veterinary surgeon may advise extra courses. Most treatments do not kill the eggs, so it is sometimes necessary to re-dose several times over a 3-month period to catch the hatching eggs.

Will neutering stop my cat from 'marking' in the home?

It has been clinically confirmed that neutering will not stop a cat from marking when the behaviour has already become established. Early castration of toms can reduce the risk of marking behaviour in that the drive to mark does not become over-stimulated and therefore an instinctive habit (see page 196). Behaviour therapy has been proved to eliminate home-marking in cats and this treatment should be implemented as soon as possible.

Will neutering stop my cat from being aggressive?

Cats that are already displaying aggressive behaviour will not cease the behaviour after neutering. However, the effects of hormone reduction in toms and queens over several months after neutering may eventually lead to a natural reduction in the drive to defend their established territory from other cats (see pages 196–197).

What is a fur ball?

The 'feline fur ball' is created by cats that are not brushed regularly, or those that obsessively groom themselves and other cats (allogrooming – see page 144). A combination of these two major factors can lead to intestinal and digestive disorders and eventually appetite problems in cats.

When hair is constantly ingested, especially by long-haired cats, it combines with natural mucus to form elongated lumps that are either regurgitated or passed through with the faeces. These are called fur balls. In acute cases, fur balls can lead to airway and intestinal blockages.

How do I give my cat a quick 'health check'?

You can use a grooming session to make a routine health check. This would include inspecting the underbelly, anal area, mouth, ears, eyes and nose. It can

* Check combs and brushes by tapping and shaking them onto a white card. This will highlight any odd specks that may be the tell-tale signs of a flea infestation. Early detection of fleas can make treatment much more effective.

Why does my neutered cat's stomach seem to be low like she is pregnant, but this appears to be permanent?

It has been suggested that in some female neutered cats being fed entirely on complete dried food diets causes them to put on this kind of weight. The underbelly fur can hang down in some cats and this gives them the appearance of being pregnant. Once this appearance has developed the cat will show the sagging underbelly look for the rest of its life. There is no reason to worry about this, but it may be advisable to control the cat's diet when the change in shape first begins to develop.

How can I give my cat liquid medicine?

The simplest method of giving cats liquid medicine requires two people. One holds the cat at the front and one at the back. Decide which person will open the cat's mouth as wide as is reasonable without causing it any distress, then quickly press a soft, plastic medicine spoon filled with the liquid onto the back of the cat's tongue, tip the medicine down, close the cat's mouth and hold it like that for a moment. Then allow the cat to take

ABOVE **A quick weekly health check can result in early detection of illness. Work through the points given in the list below during a grooming session.**

be useful to offer the cat a few tasty food treats to help make a positive association with the health check.

* Gently feel and stroke the underbelly to check for any abnormality such as growths or swellings.
* Gently draw both hands down the flanks to check for any abnormalities and lumps.
* Check that the eyes are clear and the nose clean.
* Check that the outer area of each inner ear is clean and there are no signs of any discharge.
* Open the mouth to view the teeth and gums, and to check for any unusual odour that may indicate an infection.
* Any sign of faecal stains on the hair around the anal area is an early indication of a wide range of potential health problems.

flight or, if its dignity is still intact, offer a special food treat. The key to succeeding at this is to have everything you need ready in advance and to make every action as speedy as possible with the least amount of drama.

Is there an easy way to administer tablets?

The easiest method for administering large tablets is to crush them up with the back of a dessertspoon. Then add the powder to a controlled amount of the cat's favourite food. Miss out one feed in order to make the 'medicine meal' more likely to be successful. Small tablets can be given using the same method as recommended for administering liquid medicine (see page 223), although some cats will immediately regurgitate them. If this is the case, revert to the method advised for large tablets.

How can I best look after my cat when it is poorly?

Unwell cats need a confident, minimum-fuss owner. The more fuss and anxiety given out by the owner, the more the cat will sense and worry. Offer a convalescing cat a den or igloo-type bed in a warm and quiet place. A 'comfort blanket' in the form of a soft, woollen item of old clothing scented by the owner may help.

How do I know when my cat has fleas?

Excessive scratching or frantic licking could be a sign of fleas. Check the coat for flea droppings, which look like a fine black powder at the base of the fur. Seek the advice of a veterinary surgeon as soon as possible.

How can I stop my cat from getting fleas?

Buy a flea collar each season to be worn as a preventative measure. Wash cat bedding or any soft furnishings that support a sleeping cat on a regular basis, to reduce the risk of re-infestation.

RIGHT Wearing a flea collar can help your cat to reduce the chance of an infestation. Fleas are most active in spring and summer.

LEFT Encouraging a cat to take tablets can be enhanced by careful handling and gentle throat stroking. Ideally, this is a two-person job.

How do flea collars work?

A cat flea collar is impregnated with an insecticide treatment that kills parasitic invertebrates such as fleas. This breaks the egg-laying cycle of the flea and keeps infestations at bay.

How does a course of treatment my veterinary surgeon has offered treat my cat's fleas?

Some advanced flea treatments 'immunize' the cat against flea infestations. The treatment not only kills the adults but is effective against the hatching fleas as they leave the eggs. A standard course can protect a cat for several months.

Is it best to treat for fleas just in spring and summer?

Fleas are most active reproductively in late spring and summer. However, cats can pick up fleas from other cats that are heavily infected, especially untreated feral cats, at any time of year. Outdoor cats should be treated for fleas three or four times a year to offer complete cover.

How should I deal with my cat's minor cuts and grazes?

Looking after a cat who loves the outdoors can demand some basic first aid skills. It is not unlike taking care of a child who is always coming home with

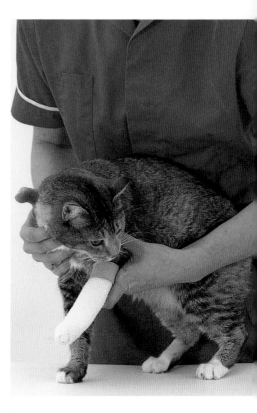

ABOVE Any serious or significant injury should be reviewed and treated by a qualified professional as soon as possible.

grazed knees and skin cuts.
- Clean minor wounds and grazes with lukewarm, boiled water to which a diluted non-phenolic antiseptic has been added. Apply to the area with a heavy-duty cottonwool ball or make-up wipe.
- It is possible to apply a mild antiseptic cream to a minor scratch or graze, but cats do tend to lick off anything foreign they find on their coat. Do not use any phenol-based antiseptic.
- Any more significant wound should be reviewed by a veterinary nurse.

What should I do when my cat has vomited?

Cats vomit easily as a protection against the ingestion of harmful substances, fur balls or inappropriate prey food. A single event should therefore not cause too much alarm. However, repeated vomiting could indicate the presence of a much more serious condition, and if this is associated with loose stools or diarrhoea can be extremely debilitating for a cat. In this instance, you should seek prompt veterinary attention as an early diagnosis can save the life of the cat.

What should I do if I believe my cat is vomiting because it has eaten a poison?

The first priority in any such incident is to identify the poisonous substance that the cat has ingested as quickly as possible. This is because the next step, if action is taken correctly, can lead to the early recovery of the cat.

It is important to recognize that the cat may in fact be suffering from the effects of various diseases or conditions. In the case of an active outdoor cat, it can be very difficult to identify the poison. Common dangers include:

• Rodent poisons, including rat pellets.
• Slug pellets.
• Poisonous plants.
• Insecticides.
• Some freshly applied wood preservatives.
• Household chemicals and paints – a cat can easily step into one of these

substances and then proceed to lick the irritant from its paws.

There are some first aid measures you can take, depending on the actual poison that the cat has taken:

To prevent your cat grooming a potentially poisonous irritant, make a temporary Elizabethan collar from cardboard and put it on the cat immediately. Use a mild shampoo and a kitchen cloth soaked in warm water to wash the contaminated coat and feet. If the poisonous contaminant can be identified, it is important to obtain the manufacturer's recommendations for treatment.

In some cases, an emetic (vomit-inducing substance), such as sodium bicarbonate, can be given. But always seek urgent advice from your veterinary practice first.

Where corrosive acids or alkalis are involved, vomiting should not be induced. Sodium bicarbonate will help to neutralize the effect of an acid; vinegar or orange juice can help to do the same for alkalis.

When sleep-inducing poisoning has occurred through ingestion of narcotic substances such as sleeping pills, white spirit, turpentine or paraffin, vomiting should be induced using sodium bicarbonate, mustard or salt water.

If the cat has eaten a seizure-inducing convulsant such as slug pellets or poisonous plants, again vomiting should be induced using sodium bicarbonate, mustard or salt water.

However, it cannot ever be over-emphasized that urgent veterinary attention is always essential if severe convulsions, collapse or acute stiffness is observed in a cat.

ABOVE **Cats should be kept well away from human medicines. Keep all medicines in a secure cupboard out of reach of pets.**

What could it mean when there is blood in my cat's urine?

This can be caused by a number of bladder and urethral infections, as well as some general feline conditions. These include feline urological syndrome and acute feline cystitis (see page 218). When this sign is first observed, it is important to have the cat examined by a veterinary surgeon at the earliest opportunity so that treatment can be applied to prevent the progress of the condition.

Are some household products highly dangerous to cats?

Household products that are dangerous to a young child are equally so for a young, inquisitive cat. It is unlikely that a cat would actively drink bleach or a paint-thinning product, for example, but a bottle or tin with a loose-fitting cap or lid could easily be knocked over by a cat searching a cupboard for a secret place to rest. The cat then steps onto spilled liquid and instinctively licks its paws clean. Such products should be safely locked away from both children and fascinated felines.

What could it mean when there is blood in my cat's faeces?

When a cat passes stools that are blood-stained this could indicate a range of causes. These include internal bleeding, poisoning and acute digestive infections. It is vital to have the cat examined by a veterinary surgeon to establish a clinical diagnosis that could lead to early and therefore successful treatment.

Why has my cat become withdrawn and nervous?

The main causes for a cat dramatically changing its behaviour are physical injury, diseases and infection, and trauma. A cat remaining in one place longer than usual, breathing heavily and erratically, or moving oddly should be examined by a veterinary surgeon as soon as possible. Any cat that appears to have had an instant 'personality change', transforming from an outgoing cat to one that is displaying withdrawn behaviour, should be treated by a feline behaviourist once physical causes have been ruled out.

My cat has eczema – how should I help?

Some cats can develop dermatological conditions like feline eczema that affect the skin and coat. These can lead to fur loss, inflammation, and dry and flaky skin. An allergic reaction to food, some materials, excessive use of insecticide-impregnated flea collars and flea dirt can all cause itchiness and skin rashes. A cat will often begin grooming excessively, only to exacerbate the condition.

It is advisable to arrange for your veterinary surgeon to undertake skin tests, and to eliminate the possibility of any external parasite being the cause of the problem.

Will homoeopathic remedies help my cat?

Homoeopathy working on humans is still questionable, when the placebo effect of a remedy can come into play. However, cats are not influenced psychologically in this way and it has yet to be proved that low concentrates of herbal extracts can have a useful effect on a cat's physical and psychological well-being.

Veterinary surgeons who try homoeopathic remedies rarely see any dramatic improvements over and above conventional medicine when treating a cat that has a physical condition and they do not protect cats from any infectious diseases. There is also a lack of any clinical evidence that homoeopathic remedies have helped to treat cats that are suffering from behavioural problems.

Should I have a cat first-aid kit?

Yes – a feline first-aid kit is an owner's physical insurance policy in case something untoward happens to their cat. The contents will not be so different from a kit designed for humans. Ideally, you will never have to use a first aid kit. Nevertheless, in the moments following an injury or accident, you will be very pleased to have access to the basic first aid needs of a companion cat.

What should be included in a feline first-aid kit?

The following set of items would be recommended by most veterinary surgeons and cat experts for inclusion in a first aid kit. They should be divided into two sets, and stored in separate sections. Never use aspirin or similar drugs.

Set 1
• Light bandages of different widths and lengths, but relevant for the size of an adult cat.

- High-quality cottonwool and cottonwool buds (avoid the type that shed small strands).
- Gauze.
- Sterile dressings.
- Roll of adhesive medical tape.
- Small roll of adhesive bandage.
- Towel (of a suitable size for holding the cat).

Set 2
- Surgical spirits.
- Table salt.
- Small tube of mild antiseptic cream or powder.
- Optical solution.

ABOVE The ideal feline first-aid kit should contain a range of utensils and dressings. The items required are listed on page 229 and below.

- Antiseptic wash.
- Mild disinfectant.
- Milk of magnesia.
- Liquid paraffin.

Instruments
- Small thermometer plus KY jelly (for ease of insertion).
- Long tweezers.
- Large and small pairs of round-tipped scissors.

What should be done with a cat at the roadside that has been in a traffic accident?

It is not generally a legal requirement to report a collision with a cat to the authorities. Nevertheless, a cat that has been involved in a road traffic accident may have a limited time to survive and so there will be an urgent need to act quickly.

1 Remove the cat from any further danger by gently placing a strong piece of cardboard or heavy-duty plastic shopping bag underneath it and carefully transferring it to a safe place.
2 If possible, check for a pulse, which can be found on the inside of the cat's thigh close to where this joins the body. It is also advisable to check whether the cat is breathing by placing a hand on its chest. If the pulse or breathing is irregular or non-existent, open the cat's mouth and bring the tongue forward. Try to check if the airway is clear.
3 If the cat appears lifeless, attempt to establish whether or not there is a heartbeat by placing two fingers on the chest behind the front legs. Any rhythm should be easily detected.
4 Gently touch the open eye to see if there is any reflex.
5 If there is evidence of heavy bleeding, locate the wound and stem any blood flow by applying pressure to the wound.
6 An injured cat will go into shock, so it important to keep it warm with a blanket or jacket.
7 Contact a veterinary surgeon immediately to arrange for a full examination.

What should I do to help my cat following treatment after a road traffic accident?

A cat convalescing from a road traffic accident would need the same peace and calmness as a human in the same situation. Some cats would sleep a great deal, using nature's way to further the healing process. However, an injured cat may attempt to achieve its normal daily routine which may involve being energetic, and this can lead to further distress and even the undoing of any surgical procedures.

It is advisable to confine a recovering cat to a single room that should include a covered litter tray, a tall scratching post, and accessible food and water. Although most active cats would be extremely frustrated by confinement, the isolation room should be used until sufficient recovery has been made.

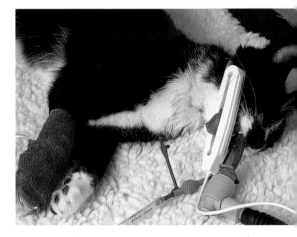

ABOVE A seriously injured cat that has been involved in a road traffic accident will need urgent medical attention.

What should I do if my cat has a bite injury?

Some basic injuries can be treated in much the same way as a child's playtime scratches. A tub of lukewarm boiled water, a little mild, non-phenolic antiseptic and an unscented wipe is usually sufficient.

A small open wound, with little or no bleeding, should first be exposed by gently clipping the fur with wet scissors (ensure clipped hairs do not enter the wound). The cleaned wound should be wiped with the antiseptic solution or dusted with antiseptic powder several times a day, because the cat will tend to over-groom the area.

Any wound that is severe, continually bleeding or that discolours in any way should be examined and attended to by a veterinary nurse in the first instance, who will be able to decide whether your veterinary surgeon should look at it.

How should I help my cat if it has a burn?

It is important to apply cold water to a heat burn as soon as possible in order to reduce the skin temperature. It is often recommended that petroleum jelly is applied to skin that has been burned, but this can irritate the sensitive area and encourage a cat to over-groom and clean it, thus damaging the skin further.

OPPOSITE **It is advisable to gently clean a small wound with a mild antiseptic solution as soon as you become aware of it.**

It is always advisable to consult your veterinary surgeon or practice nurse immediately after bathing the burn in cool water and, if possible, investigate the cause. This can range from a cat coming into contact with boiling liquids, electrical burns, domestic or industrial chemical burns, and, in the case of a white cat or one with thin hair, even sunburn, particularly on the ears and nose.

Obviously, you should switch off any electrical appliances and take reasonable care to prevent self-injury or exposure to dangerous liquids before aiding the cat.

What should I do if my cat is behaving strangely and may have an internal injury?

A cat that appears extremely unsteady on its feet or is lying down and breathing heavily may be showing signs of an internal injury or serious major organ stress. There are several steps that you should follow:

1 At the first indication of an internal injury, wrap the cat carefully in a soft cloth to enable it to be moved, then transfer it to a cat carrier cushioned with soft towelling for confinement. If the carrier is an open type, cover it with a cloth to provide some shade. If the cat is extremely agitated when first handled, take it gently by the scruff of the neck with support to its underbelly and then transfer it into a wrap-around cloth.

2 Telephone ahead to the veterinary surgery.

3 Transport the cat to the veterinary surgeon for urgent examination.

How should I help my cat if it has something stuck in its mouth?

As soon as you suspect this is the case, follow the steps below.

1 Locate a small torch or flashlight and if possible a pair of long-stemmed tweezers before attempting to restrain the cat, so that what is needed is ready in advance.
2 Quickly and confidently wrap a cloth around the cat to prevent it from struggling in panic and thus causing you injury with its claws.
3 Enlist the help of a second person to hold the cat, then open its jaws and shine the torch into its mouth.
4 If an obstruction cannot be seen or the object cannot be removed easily, take the cat to the veterinary surgery immediately for examination.

What should I do if my cat has something stuck up its nose?

Confident handling is always the key to dealing with physical mishaps with cats. Follow a similar procedure to that for looking into a cat's mouth (see above) to inspect the nasal openings closely. Take great care if you are attempting to remove a thorn or similar inanimate object from a cat's nose, as it is possible to damage the sensitive nasal passages. A cold compress can be applied to stem any bleeding. Again, if an obstruction cannot be seen or the object cannot be removed easily, the cat should be transferred to the veterinary surgery as early as possible.

How should I help my cat if he has something in his eye?

A cat with a foreign object in its eye will instinctively attempt to paw it out. This repeated action can cause further injury.

1 It may be advisable to make a temporary Elizabethan collar or wrap the cat's feet with medical tape to prevent it causing itself further injury
2 If the object has penetrated the eye, no attempt should be made to wipe it as this action could cause further injury.
3 Douse a piece of strong-fibre cotton (cottonwool could leave fibres in the eye) with lukewarm boiled water, then try to part the eyelid and gently wipe the eye from the corner outwards.
4 The cat should then be transferred to the veterinary surgery for professional examination.

Is it all right to cut out matted and knotted fur?

It can often be helpful to grooming to rid a long-haired cat of problem fur knots. The cat must be suitably restrained, so that injury to owner or cat through claws or rounded scissors cannot be caused accidentally. Bath, dry and comb the cat with a wide-toothed comb first, to ensure that the knots or matted fur cannot be unravelled or released easily, before proceeding to cut away any hairs.

OPPOSITE Great care should be taken before attempting to deal with an object or injury that has affected the eyes of a cat.

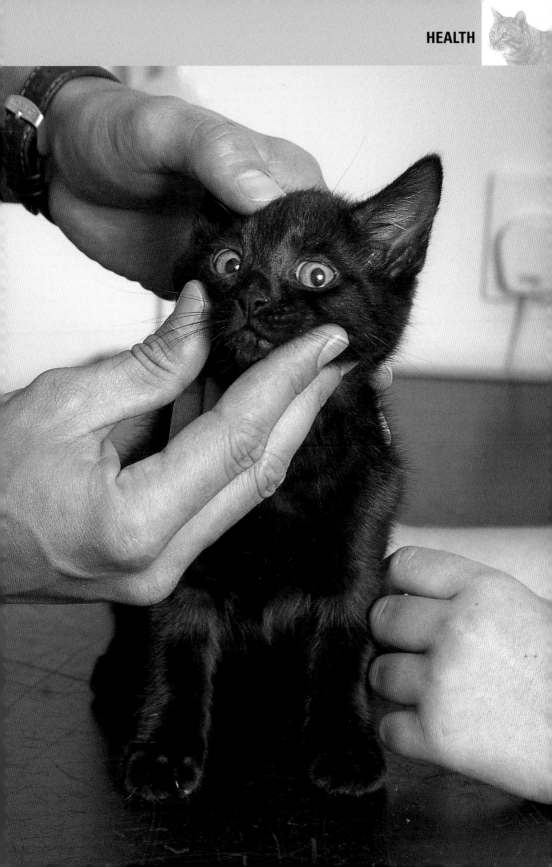

10

Infirmity

At what age is a cat considered to be old?

Cats can live to around 20 years old – even longer in some exceptional individuals. This is equivalent to a human age of 100 years, so few cats live this long.

The average lifespan for a cat is between 12 and 15 years. A cat that has reached 2 years of age has gone through the equivalent of human childhood and the teenage years and is in its twenties; cats are deemed middle-aged at about 7 years, where they are the equivalent of a human age of 40 years (see page 20). Any cat that is beyond this age can be considered to be heading for old age and feline retirement.

Some cats retain their youthfulness and seem always to want to be kittens. (Research suggests that humans inadvertently keep dogs and cats in a regression around pre-adolescence.) Other cats wish to retire gracefully and actively avoid any commotion and chaos, simply seeking out a warm place to rest and be calm.

What are the signs of ageing in cats?

There are a number of signs to look out for. The first set are obvious outward **physical** signs:
- Dark-coloured cats may gradually develop a greyish coat in old age.
- Eyes are not as bright in older cats.
- Whiskers are not so perfectly preened.
- Ears are not so quick to prick up at the slightest sound.

Infirm cats also show their age in their **movement** (or lack of it):
- Movement is less graceful and slower.
- Older cats often spend a great deal of time dozing in warm, quiet, hideaway places.
- They may move as though they are arthritic or suffering from rheumatism; occasionally a cat may have developed one or other of those conditions in a particular leg joint.

Cats may also show their age in their **eating** habits:
- Ageing cats often eat less than when they were younger – as their overall activity reduces, they are less in need of replenishment for energy.
- Conversely, some elderly cats take to 'comfort eating' – a greedy cat may put on weight with the combination of less activity and the same quantities of food on offer.

Age also shows itself in the cat's **behaviour** patterns:
- Older cats may remain in the home more and wander outdoors less, especially in the colder seasons.
- Play behaviour reduces.
- The need to rub up against, scratch and mark objects and people abates as the elderly cat leaves such youthful activities behind.

All this puts older cats on a par with most ageing owners.

Does my cat need a change of diet now that she is old?

Older, less active cats do not need high levels of protein or carbohydrates in their food. This is because they are no longer

ABOVE **Older cats show the obvious signs of ageing including slow movement, a less vibrant coat and generally subdued behaviour.**

building muscles and bone (protein) or burning up energy (carbohydrates).

If your older cat is eating a complete dried food diet, then it is time to choose the lower-protein recipe that has been developed especially for mature cats. If other foods are being offered, identify low-protein level versions and reduce the amount of food offered. By reducing the amount of food given, the carbohydrate intake will also be reduced.

What extra care can I give my cat now he is old?

Mature cats tend to spend long periods asleep or lounging in the best sun spot in a quiet room. Giving your cat a hook-on radiator bed will allow him to curl up where it is warm. Apart from peace and quiet and a mature feline diet (see opposite), there is nothing other than love and affection that you can give to an ageing cat.

It is a good idea to get your veterinary surgeon to give your old cat a general examination and thorough teeth check-up at least once a year. This frequency means that potential major organ problems can be detected early, as well as decayed or lost teeth that can make eating extremely difficult.

How can I help my old cat that has lost many teeth and seems to have difficulty eating?

An older cat that has suffered extensive tooth loss and decay will find it difficult to eat some dried foods and tough meats. Semi-moist foods are available that would be easier for a cat with a delicate mouth to consume. Look for low-protein versions of all foods, because infirm cats will be healthier on these. Canned foods can be chopped into fine pieces if necessary.

BELOW Ageing and infirm cats are often content to spend less time outdoors and will rest more in warm places indoors.

My cat is getting very old and stays inside all the time. Is this normal?

It is quite common for a mature cat to give up some of its old ways and retire to a contented indoor life. This very much depends on the personality of the individual cat, because some adventurers do not ever want to give up on adolescence and the days of chasing leaves, patrolling and competing for territory, or pouncing on unfortunate birds and unsuspecting rodents.

The majority of older cats, however, want the quiet life and like nothing better than regular, small meals and frequent opportunities to stretch out and rest in the most comfortable of places.

ABOVE **Resting periods become more and more extended as cats age. Sometimes they seem confused when they wake up.**

Is it normal for my old, once active, cat to sleep for most of the time?

It is perfectly normal for elderly or infirm cats to spend a great deal of their time resting in a favourite comfortable spot. Just as with elderly humans, cats become weaker and less active in old age. Usually, they will have spent most of their active lives expending lots of energy. So in their twilight years it will probably be something of a relief to them to take long periods of sleep somewhere quiet in between periods of sitting in an upstairs window ledge watching the world go by.

How should I call my cat now that he seems to be deaf and cannot hear me?

Deafness and infirmity can go together with cats, just as it often does with humans. Cats usually compensate for deafness by sharpening up the other senses. A deaf cat would be extremely sensitive to vibrations felt by the body and this could be used as a way of signalling to him to get his attention. The clatter of an old tin plate rattled on the floor or the fence might be detected by a hard-of-hearing cat that is close by.

Alternatively, special vibrating collars that are set off by remote control are also available. These are very useful as a way of calling cats that do not stray too far from their home as they have a fairly limited range.

My old cat seems to miss the litter tray completely. Is this due to old age?

It is possible that feline infirmity can lead to a cat becoming less than diligent about placing faeces. However, if mishaps are occurring on a regular basis it could be more a case of feline middening behaviour (see page 171). Older cats are less competitive, and it may be easier for a mature cat to register its ownership inside the home rather than outside, where it would have to challenge cats that cross into its territory.

How can I help my old cat now that his eyesight is failing?

With a reduction in any of the senses comes a compensating enhancement of the remainder. It is possible to use distinctive sound signals, such as a tinkling bell or the clicker system (see page 166), to help communicate with a cat that has failing eyesight.

Should I obtain a kitten to 'cheer up' my old cat?

The answer to this is no. Young kittens grow into adult cats, and while competition for resources might be low-key in the early kitten days, the young developing cat will soon compete with the older cat for access to food, territory and you. It is possible to stress an infirm cat by exposing it to a young, virile and athletic kitten.

Can old cats suffer from arthritis, like humans?

All vertebrate animals, including humans and cats, experience a decline in overall physical health alongside the normal ageing process. One result of this can be osteological (bone) deterioration and disease, like arthritis. Many life factors contribute to the speed of the ageing process, including early socialization, environmental issues, diet and life experience. A cat that has had a difficult time during its early socialization, been exposed to stress and eaten a less than adequate diet early in its development will be less well equipped to fight off the effects of ageing. A cat that has battled against the things a hard life can expose it to will show more physical wear and tear than a home cat that has enjoyed a privileged and protected lifestyle.

Can old cats suffer from rheumatism, like humans?

Cats experience wear and tear to muscles and joints in much the same way as humans do. There are many physical conditions, infections and diseases that are shared by all vertebrate animals. There is evidence that where an animal has evolved to survive in a climate without extremes (such as the desert cat) and is then exposed to a tough life and extreme weather in cold, wet or damp environments, it is more likely to develop rheumatoid conditions.

A reduction in exercise, a warm hearth rug and a good life is more or less all that

ABOVE **Kittens may initially stimulate older cats but eventually they mature and become competitors. They can cause older cats considerable stress.**

can be done to help a once-active cat that has slowed down because it is succumbing to the ageing process.

What exactly does pet euthanasia involve?

A cat that is sadly, but necessarily, to be euthanized is given an overdose of an anaesthetic via a hypodermic syringe by a veterinary surgeon. Vets are animal lovers too and they often find the process of euthanasia distressing – and especially emotional if they have known the cat and its owner throughout the pet's life. Some owners wish to attend the process, while others find it extremely difficult and decide to leave matters to the vet.

Whichever option you choose, you can always discuss the whole process openly with the veterinary surgeon or practice nurse beforehand. It is important to know that the euthanasia process is completely painless for the cat, and once the anaesthetic has been administered, it gently passes away.

What happens to my cat's body after euthanasia at the surgery?

Some owners wish to take away the body of their cat. Otherwise, the veterinary practice can arrange for disposal of the body through cremation. In this situation, the surgery will retain the cat until an official from the crematorium arrives to collect it.

Can I bury my cat in the garden?

It is possible to bury a cat in your garden. There are generally no regulations that have to be followed if you make this decision. Many owners dig

ABOVE Some owners find it easier to cope spiritually with their loss if they have their deceased cat buried in a pet cemetery.

a grave and then plant a rose bush or shrub on the spot to mark their cat's burial spot for many years ahead.

How do I arrange to have my cat buried in a pet cemetery?

The staff at your veterinary surgery should be able to give you details of local pet cemeteries. Alternatively, you can find them listed in business telephone directories. It is usually possible either to transport the cat's body yourself or to arrange for the veterinary practice to transfer the body to the cemetery.

Many pet cemeteries are located in peaceful rural areas and offer a range of headstones or cremation plaques to commemorate a deceased pet.

Do pets miss each other when one dies?

There is significant evidence that pets form social bonds with each other. It is not surprising, then, that the loss of animals that have experienced a long-term relationship can adversely affect the remaining pets.

Many owners have reported that their surviving companion pets exhibit behaviour changes, with some becoming introverted and withdrawn from the time of the death while others appear to take the loss with little reaction. This is more likely to occur in situations where the deceased animal has been the lead cat (or dog, or horse, in the case of these animals). A cat can react badly to the

loss of a dog, and vice versa, if they had a positive relationship with each other.

Why can I not come to terms with the loss of my cat?

It can be extremely traumatic for owners when their favourite cat is no longer around. The majority of people who do not own companion animals often fail to realize the strength of the emotional bond that can exist between owner and pet. In the case of companion cats, that bond can stretch over 20 years and the loss of a feline friend can weigh extremely heavily on a sensitive owner.

So much is missing when a cat is no longer there to greet them first thing in the morning, in the evening and forever in the kitchen, where the cat was usually to be found brushing up against them in a way guaranteed to produce a treat or some supper. It is not surprising that owners find it difficult to fill that gap in their lives.

ABOVE Sometimes a happier memory of a much-loved but deceased cat can be found in the pages of a family photograph album.

What can I do in order to come to terms with the loss of my cat?

Coming to terms with the death of a cat is often about modifying the immediate memory. It is often almost impossible not to focus on the last moments in the life of a companion animal and, by association, any illness and trauma that led to its eventual death.

Some owners find the loss of a companion animal more unbearable than the loss of a human friend or family member, due to the combination of the 'unconditional love' apparently offered by their pet and the fact that with humans it is possible to share the loss with others and discuss human life and death more openly.

It is important to allow the natural grieving process to unfold, but perhaps advisable, after a week of sadness, to switch the focus onto the happier days in the life of the cat. You could perhaps bring together photographs taken when your cat was lounging on the lawn on a balmy summer's day, or caught in action taking lazy swipes at butterflies, or sitting on the knee of a family friend or relative. Remembering those days will bring you a warm feeling and a smile, and celebrate the life you had together in a positive way.

Should I replace my dead companion cat as quickly as possible?

The answer to this question depends completely on personal factors. These include such things as whether or not the grieving process has taken place, and if your lifestyle is such that a companion animal is a vital part of it.

No two cats ever have the same personality, so it is virtually impossible to replace a cat – in just the same way as it would be impossible to replace a family member. If you decide that you are going to get a new companion, it is important not to be drawn into making comparisons between the new cat and the previous one, which will be held forever in fond memory.

Is it all right to get another cat when I am afraid it could outlive me?

This is a very difficult question to answer. You may feel guilty at this prospect, but on the positive side it could be argued that the years of companionship gained by both owner and cat – especially one

that has been adopted, having suffered the trauma and indignity of being rescued and rehomed – would probably outweigh any difficulties presented by the death of the owner.

Can I make a donation to a pet charity in memory of my cat?

This is one of the more positive ways of celebrating the life of a favourite feline friend. It might be appropriate to locate a local individual who has dedicated their life to homing rescued cats, rather than make an anonymous donation to one of the large animal organizations. A donation, however modest, will help to feed and house these unfortunate cats until a new home can be found. Doing this in memory of a dearly loved and sorely missed cat is a lovely way to remember your pet.

Do I need to provide for my cat in my will?

Providing for a cat in your will is not usually necessary. This would generally only arise if there are no living relatives who would be willing to adopt or arrange the process of rehoming your pet. However, for your own peace of mind in the meantime it might be advisable to put aside a nominal amount in your will to ensure the continued safekeeping of your loved cat.

It may also be possible to discuss the eventuality with an animal organization, which would take on the responsibility

of your cat upon your death knowing that they would be bequeathed a sum to cover costs.

ABOVE A favourite photograph of a loved family cat can help owners celebrate its life. Get the photograph enlarged and professionally framed.

How can I best celebrate the life of my cat?

The answer to this question is probably personal to the individual. However, there are several simple but effective ways in which you can commemorate the life of a dearly loved cat:

- Arrange to have a favourite photograph enlarged and professionally framed, to be given pride of place on a wall or window ledge in the room you use most in the house.

- Helping a local animal rescue organization on a fund-raising day or by making a donation is another way to celebrate the wonderful relationship you had with your pet.

- Another simple option is to focus on a special or favourite memory and write down your thoughts about it in a special book. Add drawings or photographs to the words and occasionally, in a quiet, nostalgic moment, bring it out, pour a glass of wine and toast the life and times you were fortunate enough to share.

Index

Picture Acknowledgements

Alamy/Ace Stock Limited 5 picture 10, 236; /Brand X Pictures 237 top, 247; /Webstream 134

Ardea 5 picture 9, 162, 210, 225; /John Daniels 63, 73, 75 bottom right, 75 bottom left, 78, 103 right, 116, 152, 177; /Jean Michel Labat 138, 145; /Johann de Meester 128

Bruce Coleman Collection 5 picture 8, 155, 192, 198

Corbis UK Ltd/Tom & Dee Ann McCarthy 237 bottom right, 245; /Sunset Boulevard/Sygma 27

Sylvia Cordaiy 84, 184, 244

John Daniels 113, 239

Frank Lane Picture Agency/Richard Becker 123 bottom left, 133; /Minden Pictures/M. Iwago 53 bottom left, 71; /Philip Perry 9 top, 12

Getty Images/Ross Anania 1, 137 top, 174

Octopus Publishing Group Limited 5 picture 2, 28, 30 right, 44, 53 top, 62, 94, 125; /Colin Bowling/Paul Forrester 115; /Jane Burton 5 picture 5, 86, 91, 92, 97, 98 top, 98 top centre, 98 bottom centre, 98 bottom, 99, 100 left, 100 right, 105 left, 105 right, 108, 124, 132, 140, 178, 180, 194 top right, 194 bottom right, 209, 212, 220, 224, 230, 237 bottom left, 243; /John Daniels 101; /Steve Gorton 5 picture 3, 11, 52, 60, 65, 66, 110, 130, 159, 166, 176, 196, 197; /Jerry Harpur 103 left; /Peter Loughran 15, 23, 75 top, 80; /Ray Moller 2 picture 12, 2 picture 11, 2 picture 10, 2 picture 9, 2 picture 8, 2 picture 7, 2 picture 6, 2 picture 5, 2 picture 4, 2 picture 3, 2 picture 2, 2 picture 1, 5 picture 1, 8, 9 bottom right, 10-27 top, 19, 22, 24, 25 top, 25 bottom right, 26 top, 26 bottom, 28 top right, 29 top, 29 bottom right, 29 bottom left, 30 left, 30-51 top, 31 top, 31 bottom, 32 left, 32 right, 33 top, 33 bottom, 34 top, 34 bottom, 35 top, 35 bottom, 37 top, 37 bottom, 38 left, 38 right, 39, 40 top, 40 bottom, 41, 42 top, 42 Bottom, 43, 45, 46, 47 left, 47 right, 48, 49 top, 49 bottom, 50, 51, 54-73 top, 56, 61, 76-85 top, 88-121 top, 122-135 top, 124-135 top, 138-189 top, 194-209 top, 212-235 top, 238-247 top; /Dick Polar 104; /Ron Sutherland 216; /George Taylor 117

Angela Hampton/Family Life Picture Library 5 picture 6, 5 picture 4, 18, 53 bottom right, 64, 74, 82 centre, 87, 93, 95, 121, 122, 129, 139, 144, 149, 154, 160, 165, 193 top, 206, 211 bottom left, 218, 221, 235

MPM Products Limited 102

N.H.P.A./Agence Nature 7; /Manfred Danegger 21; /Martin Harvey 82 top; /Jane Knight 90; /Gerard Lacz 5 picture 7, 136, 142, 150; /Yves Lanceau 57; /Agence Nature 153; /Eric Soder 156

Photolibrary.com/E Lauber Lon 9 bottom left

The Picture Desk Ltd./The Art Archive/Musee de Louvre Paris/Dagli Orti 17

RSPCA Photolibrary 118, 137 bottom right, 191; /Geoff du Feu 211 top, 213; /Angela Hampton 87 bottom right, 87 bottom left, 89, 96, 106, 109, 123 bottom right, 137 bottom left, 181, 189, 192 bottom right, 202, 215, 228, 231, 240; /Ken McKay 58; /Alan Robinson 214; /Louvain Woodmass 241

Solitaire Photographic/Animal Graphics 83

Warren Photographic/Jane Burton 79, 123 top, 127, 146, 193 bottom left, 199, 204, 205, 208, 211 bottom right, 223, 226, 232

Acknowledgements

Dedication This book is dedicated to (Cat)herine, my lovely wife, who actively helped me with aspects of research for this book.

Author's acknowledgements I would like to express my sincere thanks to my veterinary colleague, Michael Clarke MRCVS, for his help with some of the more unusual feline treatment details. I also acknowledge the indirect help of my clients (and their cats) who are unusually dedicated to asking questions about their 'feline friends', or in a non judgmental way, with their 'problem pet', or 'replacement child', replacement partner or replacement friend. I continue to learn so much from my clinical work with cats.

My thanks are especially due to Sue Foster who became a friend and allowed me to photograph and observe her two wonderful cats, Max and Mim, both for my Granada TV series and, in a secondary sense, for the benefit of this book.

My genuine thanks go to Sarah Widdicombe for her many excellent questions regarding my text in the period leading up to last Christmas. My gratitude goes to Trevor Davies who kindly commissioned me to write this book, one of the most enjoyable for me to be creative about in twenty five years of being a published author.

Any reader is welcome to contact me on drdavidsands@aol.com or through www.problempets.co.uk http://www.problempets.co.uk with regard to this book or any additional questions relating to cat behaviour.

Publisher's acknowledgements
Executive editor Trevor Davies
Editor Alice Bowden
Executive art editor Geoff Fennell
Design 'Ome Design
Senior production controller Manjit Sihra
Picture manager Liz Fowler